Ethics

This book examines ethics at the intersection of law and justice. If law and justice are concerned with collectively establishing the general terms on which the plurality called "we" share the earth as social beings, then ethics concerns the individual Self's particular moral relationship with the Other. Law, the acknowledged offspring of politics, represents the kind of might that most people accept as legitimate, at least most of the time. Justice, on the other hand, is supposed to vigilantly stand guard over law: to protect us against its biases and excesses, or, at the very least, to rise up and reproach the law whenever it permits or encourages injustice. But what if the belief that a particular legally authorized state of affairs is "just" – a common enough feeling, especially amongst the privileged – or even "unjust" and in need of correction, were itself in need of a vigilant guardian? This book argues that ethics can and should stand guard over whatever image of justice and/or just law one happens to believe in. The book thus attempts to steer a perilous course between two looming moral hazards: ethics interpreted as the rational production of ethically correct behavior (as in Kant) and ethics interpreted as the spontaneous eruption of pre-rational compassion for the suffering of the Other, come what may (as in Levinas). In the end, the book characterizes ethical life in the law as the more-or-less constant experience of the paradoxical nature of this choice – a feeling of inescapable personal responsibility for the fate of the Other. Based on the author's well-established expertise in the area, this book will appeal to students, scholars, and others with interests in legal theory and moral and political philosophy.

Louis E. Wolcher is the Charles I. Stone Professor Emeritus at the University of Washington Law School.

Part of the New Trajectories in Law series
series editors
Adam Gearey, *Birkbeck College, University of London*
Colin Perrin, Commissioning Editor, Routledge

Ethics
New Trajectories in Law
Louis E. Wolcher

For information about the series and details of previous and forthcoming titles, see www.routledge.com/New-Trajectories-in-Law/book-series/NTL

A GlassHouse Book

Ethics
New Trajectories in Law

Louis E. Wolcher

LONDON AND NEW YORK

First published 2021
by Routledge
2 Park Square, Milton Park, Abingdon, Oxon OX14 4RN

and by Routledge
52 Vanderbilt Avenue, New York, NY 10017

Routledge is an imprint of the Taylor & Francis Group, an informa business

© 2021 Louis E. Wolcher

The right of Louis E. Wolcher to be identified as author of this work has been asserted by him in accordance with sections 77 and 78 of the Copyright, Designs and Patents Act 1988.

All rights reserved. No part of this book may be reprinted or reproduced or utilised in any form or by any electronic, mechanical, or other means, now known or hereafter invented, including photocopying and recording, or in any information storage or retrieval system, without permission in writing from the publishers.

Trademark notice: Product or corporate names may be trademarks or registered trademarks, and are used only for identification and explanation without intent to infringe.

British Library Cataloguing-in-Publication Data
A catalogue record for this book is available from the British Library

Library of Congress Cataloging-in-Publication Data
Names: Wolcher, Louis E., author.
Title: Ethics : new trajectories in law / Louis E. Wolcher.
Description: Milton Park, Abingdon, Oxon ; New York, NY : Routledge, 2021. | Series: New trajectories in law | Includes bibliographical references and index.
Identifiers: LCCN 2020038611 (print) | LCCN 2020038612 (ebook) | ISBN 9780367356545 (hardback) | ISBN 9780429343834 (ebook)
Subjects: LCSH: Legal ethics. | Ethics.
Classification: LCC K123 .W65 2021 (print) | LCC K123 (ebook) | DDC 174/.3—dc23
LC record available at https://lccn.loc.gov/2020038611
LC ebook record available at https://lccn.loc.gov/2020038612

ISBN: 978-0-367-35654-5 (hbk)
ISBN: 978-0-429-34383-4 (ebk)

Typeset in Times New Roman
by Apex CoVantage, LLC

For the angry ones who are also the kindly ones

Great Goddesses,
Spirits hard to pacify.
All that makes up Man's moving story
Is theirs to govern and dispense.

Aeschylus, *Eumenides* (1906: 335)

Contents

List of figures	ix
Acknowledgments	x

1 Towards an ethics writ large   1

On ethics writ small 1
Introducing the possibility of an ethics writ large 5
Telling and urging 10
In the beginning was the deed 14
Beginning at the ending 18

2 From *ethōs* to ethics   23

From custom to character to duty 23
The codependency of Is *and* Ought *as an elective*
   affinity 27
The untranslatability of metaphysical statements in
   ethics 35
Three cases: compassionless reason, reasonable
   compassion, and reason versus compassion 40

3 The burden of caring   44

The leading question 44
Towards a phenomenological interpretation of reason
   and compassion in ethics 46
"Gninnigeb eht ta nigeb" – George Oppen 52
Responsibility versus presponsibility: herein of
   Levinas 57
The politics of ethics writ large 61

viii   *Contents*

4   Ethical doubts about justice   65

The hope for justice 65
The force of law 69
Justice's guardianship over law 73
*The shabbiness of law compared to the wonderfulness
    of justice 76*
The problem of fidelity to law in a relativistic age 79
The customary agreeableness of justice 85
The suspicious wordiness of reason 90

**5   A concluding anecdote about the difference between
     ambiguity and treachery**   95

"But this is *a pipe": a law professor's anecdote 95*
The indeterminacy thesis 97
Deconstruction 98
*The treachery of ambiguity versus the ambiguity of
    treachery 100*
The ethics of self-treachery 104

References   106
Index   115

Figures

4.1	The triangle of law, justice, and ethics	67
4.2	*Dike and Adikia* (Justice and Injustice)	77
4.3	"How to Escape the Draft"	87
5.1	*La Trahison des images* ("The Treachery of Images")	96
5.2	A duck-rabbit	101

Acknowledgments

Permission to use portions of the following previously published material is gratefully acknowledged:

> Louis E. Wolcher, "The Ethical Turn in Critical Legal Thought," in E Christodoulidis, R Dikes & M Goldoni, *Research Handbook on Critical Legal Theory* (Edward Elgar, Cheltenham, UK, 2019), pp. 181–200, © The Editors and Contributors Severally 2019. Reproduced with permission of the Licensor through PLSclear.

Permission to use the image shown in Figure 5.1 is also gratefully acknowledged:

René Magritte, "The Treachery of Images," 1929
© 2020 C. Herscovici/Artists Rights Society (ARS), New York

1 Towards an ethics writ large

When I think of a categorical imperative I know at once what it contains. For, since the imperative contains, beyond the law, only the necessity that the maxim [a person's subjective principle of action] be in conformity with this law, while the law contains no condition to which it would be limited, nothing is left with which the maxim of action is to conform but the universality of a law as such; and this conformity alone is what the imperative properly represents as necessary. There is, therefore, only a single categorical imperative and it is this: *act only in accordance with that maxim through which you can at the same time will that it become a universal law*.

Immanuel Kant (1996: 73)

Thought wants to be woken one day by the memory of what has been missed, and to be transformed into teaching.

Theodor Adorno (2005: 81)

On ethics writ small

It would be tempting (but wrong) to suppose that a book entitled *Ethics: New Trajectories in Law*, as this one is, must be concerned with legal ethics in the pragmatic sense that practicing lawyers use the term. Sometimes called "professional responsibility," legal ethics writ small in this way has been defined by three leading legal ethicists as the "principles of conduct that members of the legal profession are expected to observe in their legal practice" (Pirsig, Glendon, & Alford, 2020). Although their contents have changed over time, and differ somewhat from jurisdiction to jurisdiction, the principles themselves generally deploy the language of duty, obligation, and prohibition ("ought" and "ought not," "shall" and "shall not," "may" and "may not") in an attempt to regulate the day-to-day conduct of practicing lawyers. For example, Rule 3.1 of the American Bar Association's *Model Rules of Professional Conduct* demands, *à la* the Decalogue, that

2 Towards an ethics writ large

lawyers "shall not bring or defend a proceeding, or assert or controvert an issue therein, unless there is a basis in law and fact for doing so that is not frivolous." And so forth and so on, in page after page of statements cataloguing the ethical duties of lawyers to clients, to the public, and to the legal system as a whole. Meanwhile, other similarly worded codes of conduct tell judges (ABA, 2018), law enforcement officers (IIT, 1991), public officials and employees (IIT, 2011), legislators (HR, 2011), and even law professors (Rhode, 2006) how and how not to behave if they want to be seen as ethically correct members of their respective professions.

It would also be tempting (but wrong) to suppose that any self-respecting work of legal philosophy having the word "ethics" in its title, as this one does, must somehow concern itself with analyzing, and possibly criticizing, one or more extralegal norms, principles, and/or character traits that purport to impose rational, other-regarding moral limits on individuals whose otherwise lawful actions threaten to injure others. The latter expectation was set long ago by classical ethical theorists such as Aristotle, Kant, and Bentham, who also happen to be the intellectual ancestors of the three major schools of ethical thought in vogue today: virtue ethics, deontological ethics, and teleological ethics, respectively.

Despite their many differences, most modern versions of these three schools of thought actually wage war against the same enemy: lawless liberty, defined as the absolute freedom or license to do as one pleases. The English philosopher Thomas Hobbes identified this common enemy with wholly unrestrained negative liberty – "the [total] absence of externall Impediments: which Impediments may oft take away part of a mans power to do what hee would; but cannot hinder him from using the power left him" – and famously argued that in a "state of nature" its consequence would be "that there be no Propriety, no Dominion, no *Mine* and *Thine* distinct; but only that to be every mans, that he can get; and for so long, as he can keep it" (1914: 66). While Hobbes's younger contemporary, John Locke, had a much rosier view of the primordial human capacity for decent, other-regarding behavior, he too worried that lawless liberty, if left completely unrestrained, would greatly increase people's unhappiness (1939a: 334).

Arguments such as these are normally associated with the machinations of political philosophy, not ethics. That is because the intellectuals who have felt most acutely the need to defeat lawless liberty's claimed natural right to absolute individual freedom tend to be those who are struggling to solve two interrelated theoretical problems: (1) how to justify the existence of the state, especially the liberal state, and (2) how to properly confine and restrain that state's "public" power to enforce coercive limits, via rules of law and the legal system, on the "private" behaviors of individuals and groups. According to the usual way of drawing the distinction between

Towards an ethics writ large 3

the public and private spheres, legal commands are public and therefore ultimately political in origin, whereas ethical commands are private and therefore solely a matter of individual conscience. That this way of thinking contains a grain of truth derives from the observation that state officials can imprison or mulct you in damages for violating the law, but not, generally speaking, for committing unethical acts.

Of course, there remains the knotty problem of how to use the public/private binary to classify the earlier-noted professional codes of behavior – not to mention the "corporate ethics codes" that many businesses have adopted by analogy (see Wolcher, 2011) – given that a person can be *publicly* delicensed and/or *lawfully* deprived of a living (i.e. fired) for violating them. There is also the theoretical difficulty of whether it is even possible in the first place to draw a coherent, apolitical distinction between the public and private spheres: a much-mooted point in critical legal theory (Kairys, 1990), critical race theory (Delgado, 1995), and feminist legal theory (Weisberg, 1993).

That said, however, the Hobbesian bogeyman of lawless liberty makes an appearance in ethical discourse, too, and not just in discussions of politics and law. For the term "lawless liberty" is in fact ambiguous. In traditional political theory it connotes a *society-wide* state of anarchy – the complete absence of any government, including any enforceable legal rules, capable of externally constraining the behavior of individuals and groups by force or threat of force. In traditional ethical theory, on the other hand, it refers specifically to *individuals* whose behaviors towards others remain completely ungoverned by any rationally defensible internal criterion for deciding what is and is not morally permissible; a case in point is Locke's quasi-authoritarian distinction between actions based solely on personal "enthusiasm" (bad) and actions guided by something he called the "true light in the mind" (good) (1939a: 396–402).

The possibility that a person's moral enthusiasm might gainsay their rational moral understanding in a given ethically-charged situation (or vice versa) brings into view the relationship between these two potentially contradictory affective states and the phenomenon that we call *power*: the power, that is, to effectively bend or unbend events as they flow through the being-together of Self and Other in the ethical present. Conversation about power in everyday life tends to dwell on the who "has" it rather than on what kind of thing power *as such* is, and how it manifests itself before, during, and after someone is said to "have" it. Fortunately, there is a another – and for present purposes, better – way to think about power as a phenomenon in its own right. "Power," said the French philosopher and social theorist Michel Foucault, "is not to be taken to be a phenomenon of one individual's consolidated and homogeneous domination over others, or

4 *Towards an ethics writ large*

that of one group or class over others." According to his oft-quoted methodological statement,

> Power must be analyzed as something which circulates, or rather as something which only functions in the form of a chain. It is never localized here or there, never in anybody's hands, never appropriated as a commodity or piece of wealth. Power is employed and exercised through a net-like organization. And not only do individuals circulate between its threads; they are always in the position of simultaneously undergoing and exercising this power. They are not only its inert or consenting target; they are always also the elements of its articulation. In other words, individuals are vehicles of power, not its point of application.
>
> (1980: 98)

The power of law is essentially the same. The proximate phenomenal cause of seeing law as public and ethics as private is generally not the discovery of some deep ontological truth, but rather the viewer's own political inclinations. More to the point, it is also a personal choice: a personal *ethical* choice, in fact. Public and private, the political and the ethical, converge in the body and mind of any individual who enjoys the practical legal power to let others prosper or fail, suffer or not suffer, live or die. As Foucault suggests, this happens not just in police work and other "public" callings, but also any time "private" individuals exercise their legal rights or privileges, especially if doing so will hurt or disadvantage someone else. Which is to say, it happens pretty much all the time. It is a profoundly true tautology to say that in civil society everyone who acts lawfully is *ipso facto* a kind of law-doer – a kind of undercover policeman upholding legal normalcy.

In marshaling their assorted arguments against lawless liberty's claimed natural or theological right always to pursue its own personal convenience, virtue ethics, deontological ethics, and teleological ethics all place their quintessential ethical agents into the same hypothetical temporal situation. To be precise, each of their ethical protagonists is always just on the verge of acting in a present moment wherein the actor's subsequent actions have not *yet* produced any ethically questionable results, either good or bad. What should the protagonist do, then? What kind of future is ethically permitted or required? Lodged in what seems to be a pre-ethical present moment, the agent of virtue[1] ethics has already carefully cultivated his or her moral character to respond to events in the right way (Aristotle, 1934: 95); the agent of deontological[2] ethics knows how to derive and recognize his or her moral duties from universal rules and then to perform them no matter what (Kant, 1996: 73, 80, 85); and the agent of teleological[3] ethics knows how to identify and quantify (somehow) all the social consequences, good and bad, of each course of action available to him or her, and then to choose the one that promises to harvest the largest net amount of goodness over badness, or at least the smallest net amount of badness (Bentham, 1939: 792).

Thus, in one way or another all three schools of ethical thought, together with countless variations and modifications of them in the philosophical literature, have preconditioned the average reader to believe that a book about ethics (1) *should* be about how we (2) *should* plan in advance to act towards others in order to live our lives in a way that (3) *should* be seen as morally admirable by everyone.

The theme of the present volume is indeed individual ethics in relation to law and justice. The phrase "individual ethics in relation to" is meant to imply, among other things, that an action's being widely accepted as lawful and just does not insulate it from individual ethical scrutiny, just as its being widely accepted as unlawful and unjust does not automatically make it unethical. Moreover, the investigations in this book have refused to accept any moral or editorial authority that might be validly inferred from the foregoing triumvirate of "shoulds." This book is: (1) not about the other-regarding norms that individuals should follow or the character traits they should emulate; (2) not about how individuals should plan to behave towards others; and (3) not about what everyone should admire as morally upright conduct. Instead of demanding or offering "correct" answers to these sorts of questions, these investigations are motivated by a different kind of ethical *should*.

Introducing the possibility of an ethics writ large

"Know thyself" (*gnōthi seauton*): so read a motto inscribed in the forecourt of the Temple of Apollo at Delphi. The Frankfurt School philosopher and critical social theorist Theodor Adorno leant a distinctly ethical coloration to this ancient injunction when he said, in his 1951 book *Minima Moralia: Reflections from a Damaged Life*, "The self-criticism of reason is its truest morality" (2005: 74). The "morality of thought," he wrote several pages later, entails "a procedure that is neither entrenched nor detached, neither blind nor empty, neither automatic nor consequential" (2005: 126). Presumably, this procedure would have to proceed from reason's *ex ante* moral[4] choice to remain nondogmatic, nonjudgmental, and, above all, open to being surprised by what it discovers about *itself* in relation to its subject matter. Not itself alone, mind you, not itself as a self-enclosed monad, but rather itself *qua* the unity of Self-and-Other thought together.

It is certainly true that Adorno's ethical procedure looks inconsistent with Kant's celebrated dictum that "thoughts without content are empty, intuitions without concepts are blind" (1998: 193–94). But that would be troubling only if reason insists on squeezing everything real into its concept, leaving behind no ethically problematic remainder. For Kant, the possibility of acquiring empirically true knowledge about the world depended on whether reason's

6 Towards an ethics writ large

inward gaze – its "critique of pure reason" – could discover *a priori* true knowledge about its very own categories and concepts. Later on, his "critique of practical reason" made the possibility of individual morality also depend on reason's acquisition of *a priori* knowledge about an alleged inner truth: namely, the Categorical Imperative in one (or all) of its various forms.[5]

An *a priori* truth, for Kant, is the condition of the possibly of something else: experience, for example, or morality. Its *expression* is therefore seen as gospel-like: an idealized something that should be held tight as unassailable, so to speak, by all rational subjects before, during, and after any of their actual experiences of the world. Morality seen as absolute law-abidingness, for example, acknowledges as morally real only what the law is already prepared to recognize as "relevant" to its operations. Like blinders on a mule, such a truth at once orients (good news) *and* obscures (bad news) the moral vision of the creature who clings to it as gospel.

Now is not the time to parse the Categorical Imperative or to quibble with Kant's norm-based approach to deciding what sort of mental calculations, exactly, ethics demands. That would cede too much authority too soon to the insistent claims of rule-governed normativity. Given how easy it is to fool yourself into thinking you *are* absolutely right about something that you *feel* certain about, we should simply acknowledge that Kant did us all the inestimable favor of elevating self-criticism in the moral sphere to the very highest rank.

But what if one suspects, in addition, that what is decisive in all honest thought, perhaps most of all in ethics, is what Adorno called "the critical analysis of categorical intuition" (Adorno & Benjamin, 1999: 85)? Categorical intuition is supposed to be what brings sensible experience into direct contact with our concepts; it allows us to understand and say, for example, that the big, neighing quadruped standing next to us is a "horse" and not a "cat." In short, categorical intuition is the name of a mysterious inner process that (somehow) allows us to perceive things "as" the kind of thing that our concepts have already conditioned us (somehow) to recognize.

The previous sentence's parenthetical "(somehow)s" are very important. They foreshadow two interrelated themes that bear directly on this book's interpretation of ethics in relation to law and justice: (1) the social and historical production and development of the categories that we take for granted as normal in everyday life and (2) the intimate relationship between categorical intuition (aka "knowledge") and power. We will elaborate on these themes in subsequent chapters. But it is worth mentioning one particularly noteworthy aspect of their relevance to ethics right now: people's categories cause them to be unaware of or indifferent to what repeated applications of the categories *exclude*.

The sphere of the conceptually excluded (and therefore the unrecognized) in ethics, law, and justice will henceforth be called the "remainder." What

Towards an ethics writ large 7

if the self-criticism of categorical intuition shows that ethical discourse in the context of law and justice always *does* leave behind many troubling, unassimilated remainders? Certain unfiltered, unacknowledged realities – especially the brutal realities of persistent, unnoticed human suffering – that even the best and most reasonable ethical categories do not authorize us to care about?

Kant thought that reality as it is in itself is an utterly inscrutable realm (noumenon[6]) within which transcendental reason discovers, and practical reason applies, its own categories and concepts to sensible experience (phenomenon[7]). Hegel, one of Kant's earliest successors, united the real and the ideal by trying to think them both together as elements in a single temporal process. Hegel, too, did us all the great favor of raising the nonidentity of an object with its concept to the highest rank, an idea that sits right alongside reason's Kantian commitment to the importance of self-criticism. Instead of being cast as reason's mysterious background milieu, after Hegel reality took on the role of an *agent provocateur* to reason's complacent sluggishness in response to change.

For Hegel, history is constantly producing certain unthought remainders that reason has difficulty reconciling with its existing concepts. Like Heraclitus, his favorite Greek thinker – the one who said, "We step and do not step into the same rivers" (1987: 35) – Hegel believed that nothing is ever completely at rest, and that everything is always becoming something different from what it was just a moment ago. Reason responds to the fact that historical reality is always changing by means of a diachronic inner movement that Hegel called the dialectic. Unlike Kant, Hegel realized that historical change is always producing extra-conceptual remainders. Although this insight was perhaps his greatest gift to thought, the gift had strings attached, for he also believed that not all remainders are created equal. Like the pigs in Orwell's *Animal Farm*, some remainders are more equal, more deserving of recognition than others (1995: 149).

On the one hand, dialectical thought makes every concept elastic enough to accommodate its antithesis through an active, humanly produced synthesis that takes account of any historical changes important enough for categorical intuition to notice on the basis of its existing concepts. But on the other hand, littler changes in reality also generate their own remainders, even as our concepts are expanding to incorporate all the big changes. Hegelianism authorizes reason to dismiss these little remainders as unimportant, since they are made up of a plethora of insignificant subjective reactions lying too far beneath the dignity of reason to be worthy of rational synthesis. The dialectic sweeps them under the rug of progress, which is the name that reason gives to its historical journey towards the promised land of the Absolute Idea.

8 *Towards an ethics writ large*

It is important to understand that Hegel's peripatetic dialectical maneuverings (*thesis – antithesis – synthesis*) are conducted exclusively by reason. The influence of the subjective feeling of conviction, like all other nonrational states in ethical decision-making, he denigrates as mere "ethical subjectivism" (1967: 94–103). This means that Hegelian synthesis synthesizes only what reason is prepared to notice and absorb, like a sponge absorbing water. But at any given moment of time there is always more water in reality than the sponge of a concept can absorb. What about the water that is left over? According to Albert Camus's trenchant (albeit unsystematic) objection to Hegelianism, unimportant remainders might be worthy of ethical notice, too, if only one is prepared to look at them without blinking (1965: 177).

The inevitability of progress in Hegel's system manages to unite three normative concepts – ethics, law, and justice – in the total "ethical life" (*Sittlichkeit*) of the community (1967: 319 n.75). We will return to this notion of *Sittlichkeit* in Chapter 2. But for now it should be noted that Hegel's theory of a *unified* normative sphere bears a strong family resemblance to a commonly held – indeed axiomatic – popular belief about the proper relationship amongst the three formal elements of that sphere: law, justice, and ethics. We will call this belief the Axiom of Legal Progress. Like all axioms, it requires no proof but is taken for granted as self-evidently true. One might even say that the axiom expresses a kind of Categorical Imperative for those who have internalized its message.

The Axiom of Legal Progress

The ethically correct enforcement of just law is always good and desirable.

The Axiom interprets the trilateral relationship amongst law, justice, and ethics as mutually constitutive and self-reinforcing. Seen from the point of view of the Axiom, *law* is to *justice* as a sinner is to one who is saved, since on its face the text praises only the enforcement of law that is or has become just. *Ethics*, in turn, is to the goal of enforcing just law as a morally punctilious servant is to its master, for the Axiom assigns to ethics the subsidiary role of merely being correct in the *way* that just law is enforced. Read in this way, the Axiom is actually quite narrow. Although it might be read to imply that the pursuit of legal justice by unethical means is bad, it says nothing about the goodness and desirability of enforcing *unjust* law – or more to the point, reaching an unjust result – by ethically correct means.

In short, the Axiom of Legal Progress does not address the question whether people have what legal philosophers call a duty of "fidelity" to laws

Towards an ethics writ large 9

that produce injustice – a theme to which we will return in Chapter 4. Instead, the Axiom's implication that there exists a moral and a legal duty to obey and/or enforce *just* laws seems so obvious that most people would say that it requires no argument to support it. Who, other than an irredeemable miscreant, could be against the enforcement of just law by ethically proper means?

Who indeed. So limited and beguilingly commonsensical is this idea that even the most jaded moral agnostics and pessimists would probably concur in the practical desirability of the Axiom – even if only for the same crassly utilitarian reason that the atheist Voltaire gave for wanting his attorney, his tailor, his servants, and his "wife" (he never married) to believe in God: "I fancy that as a result I shall suffer from less theft and less cuckoldry" (1994: 190).

The Axiom of Legal Progress bestows praise and encouragement on human actions that aim to achieve justice in the "correct" way. It calls the pursuit of justice through law good and desirable so long as the means used are counted as correct according to some rational calculus of correctness that has been derived from another source: namely, ethics. For example, many (or most) people would probably object on ethical grounds if a prosecutor fabricated evidence to convict defendants of crimes that they actually committed. The (just) end does not justify the (unethical) means, they would probably say.

Lest we be tempted to prematurely pronounce judgment on the truth or wisdom of the Axiom, it is important to note that the relationship between the terms "*ethically correct enforcement*" and "*just law*" is internal, not external.[8] Since their definitions are not supplied, and in fact have always been highly contested, this means that they are connected to one another solely by the way they may be defined and applied in the future, rather than by the existence of some inherent metaphysical kinship between the beings or states of affairs to which the terms refer. This is not a fatal omission, however, since this is not a book about how to recognize or achieve the best possible outcomes for law and justice. On the contrary, the book's principal argument is that there is much, much more to ethics than being ethically correct, legally correct, and fully just, and moreover, that the vapid comfort we sometimes derive from agreeing with one another about nostrums like the Axiom of Legal Progress can easily produce ethical monstrosities.

The emotional comfort we gain from swearing fealty to the Axiom is capable of producing monstrosities because the Axiom's terms are semantically empty signifiers. If laws aimed at eliminating racism and its effects have often been praised as just, so too have laws aimed at reinforcing blood-and-soil ethnic nationalism. Indeed, it is highly likely that *any* regime that is inclined to tout the marvelous justice of its laws and legal system would also be inclined to agree wholeheartedly with the Axiom of Legal Progress. That is to say, the Axiom would in all likelihood appeal to pretty much *every*

10   *Towards an ethics writ large*

regime in world history precisely because it is empty enough to accommodate just about any use of law to achieve the ends of the state.

In his 1966 magnum opus *Negative Dialectics*, Adorno called reason's relentless, power-hungry attempt to completely identify its concepts with reality "the untruth of identity." He wrote the book from the disillusioned perspective of a Marxist who had witnessed one horror after another committed by human beings in the name of instrumental reason: mass slaughter in the trenches of World War I, the Armenian genocide, Stalin's show trials, World War II, Auschwitz, the Soviet Gulag, the detonation of atomic bombs in Hiroshima and Nagasaki, the Vietnam War, to name but a few. Turning his back on the disastrous historical quest for a unanimous interpretation of reality, especially in the political and moral spheres, Adorno cut the Hegelian dialectic down to size by showing that there is always something important, or potentially important, omitted or excluded by reason's single-minded drive for unity:

> The name of dialectics says no more, to begin with, than that objects do not go into their concepts without leaving a remainder, that they come to contradict the traditional norm of adequacy. Contradiction is not what Hegel's absolute idealism was bound to transfigure it into: it is not of the essence in a Heraclitean sense. It indicates the untruth of identity, the fact that the concept does not exhaust the thing conceived.
> (1973: 5)

At its core, Adorno's negative dialectics is driven by reason's recognition – or better still, its admission to itself – that a concept can never exhaust the thing conceived. Marx's dialectical materialism – a progressive offspring of the marriage between philosophical materialism and Hegel's philosophical idealism – has no room in it for remainders that do not matter to history's inevitable journey towards a class-free society. Negative dialectics is different. It holds that a concept is like a net through which small fish will always escape, and that a concept usually captures only what it sets out to find – what it considers to be "big fish." But little fish are not nothing. They are what remains in the sea after all the big fish have been netted. *Pari passu*, a "negative ethics" (our phrase, not Adorno's) would be driven by reason's admission to itself that what happens to the little fish matters, too, even if no rational concept or category is prepared to argue their case – only a pre- or post-rational feeling of compassionate concern for the Other.

Telling and urging

We intend to heed Adorno's advice over Kant's and Hegel's when it comes to thinking about all the little fish that remain unacknowledged after reason

Towards an ethics writ large   11

has gathered what it calls "big fish" and compressed them together, like fish paste, into the form of an authoritative saying. The present investigations might therefore be called a negative ethics or an ethics of the remainder, or, better still, an ethics writ large. On the subject of ethics in relation to law and justice, this book eschews the rational quest for *a priori* knowledge (Kant) and/or the Absolute Idea at the end of history (Hegel). Like Adorno, it will avoid the comforts of self-certainty in order to blaze an unmarked middle path between extremes, and for the same reason. If the self-criticism of reason is its truest morality, as Adorno says, then perhaps its most urgent task is to prepare itself to shut up and let the murmurs of the remainder be heard.

On the one hand, an ethics of compassionless reason loudly *tells* us to resist the temptations of immediate self-interest, and then *tells* us what is right for us to do or forbear from doing. Reason's demand that we suppress or discount the gratifications of immediate self-interest in our dealings with others is understandable, of course, given that reason has traditionally considered selfish, lawless liberty to be its greatest enemy. Ethical norms are like bullets, on this view – means to the end of killing the beast of egotism run amok.

On the other hand, an ethics of unreasonable compassion soundlessly *urges* us to be kind to the Other, no matter what. The feeling of compassion does not tell people to be kind, but rather urges it into being by (somehow) provoking acts of kindness, however unreasonable. Indeed, the strongly felt phenomenon of compassion at its core seems strangely impervious to reason's arguments for why it should not exist in "inappropriate" situations. Experience teaches that compassion tends to mutely persist through time despite it's having been rationally condemned according to the normative binary *appropriate/inappropriate*. At its limit, the concept of compassion represents an attempt to think what the writer Vasily Grossman called "The private kindness of one individual towards another; a petty, thoughtless kindness; an unwitnessed kindness. Something we could call senseless kindness. A kindness outside of any system of social or religious good" (1985: 408).

The distinction between reasonable telling and compassionate urging seems, at first blush, to be a productive one, especially since it closely tracks the familiar Platonic distinction between reason (trustworthy) and emotion (untrustworthy). On closer inspection, however, the boundary line it draws between rational ethics and an ethics based on compassion shows itself to be a porous one, at best. It is porous because practical reason, too, is in the business of *urging*, not just telling; just as compassion, once it has urged an act kindness, generally likes to *tell* us, if only in an inner voice, about how decent it is.

Take rational ethics. Reason not only tells, but also urges us to suppress all other conscious urges, including unreasonable feelings of compassion, in order to do its bidding. Ever fond of reason and ever suspicious of emotion,

12 *Towards an ethics writ large*

tradition comes down heavily in favor of the head over the heart in matters of ethics. An article in the hoary Macmillan *Encyclopedia of Philosophy*, for example, defines philosophical ethics (sometimes called metaethics) as the rational inquiry into general ways of life and "rules of moral conduct" (Abelson & Nielsen, 1967: 81–82). As for the role of compassion in this inquiry, ever since Plato wrote his famous allegory of the charioteer (*Phaedrus* 246a-254e), traditional thinking about ethics – especially ethics in relation to law and politics – has claimed that the only proper relationship between reason and compassion is akin to that between an intelligent teamster and an unruly horse. Reason should come first, in the form of rigorous self-control; compassion second, but only *after* reason has harnessed and steered it in the morally correct direction.

Over the centuries, philosophers as notable and varied as Seneca,[9] Spinoza,[10] and Kant[11] have gone out of their way to criticize compassion as a dangerous moral weakness that clouds reason's capacity to recognize what the correct performance of moral duty requires. Eventually, both Rousseau and Nietzsche would launch vigorous assaults on compassion's main line of defense by trashing its altruistic self-image. "I feel your pain" became, to their way of thinking, "It gives *me* a lift to feel and say that I feel your pain." True, in the *Second Discourse*, Rousseau began his analysis of compassion for another's suffering by praising it, if only in the irreal context of a so-called pre-social state of nature. But he would go on to assert that organized society had warped compassion, along with every other virtue, into just another ignoble expression of the status-seeking social individual's feeling of superiority, or self-love (*l'amour propre*) (1993a: 95–96). Whereas Nietzsche, for his part, would scorn compassion's pride in its own selflessness as delusional, characterizing it as yet another manifestation of the will to power (1968: 199).

Traditional ethical formulas such as the Golden Rule and the Categorical Imperative neglect compassion altogether, justifying their injunctions to act with decency towards others by overtly or covertly appealing to rational self-interest. In particular, each formula offers the individual compensation for good deeds in the present by promising a future full of law-governed normative reciprocity on the basis of the universalization of an abstract norm. The oft-cited rule to do unto others as you would have them do unto you explicitly dangles future rewards before the actor, at least so long as enough people follow it; whereas Kant's injunction to act as if the maxim of your action were to become a general law of nature would appeal to no one unless they believed that universal obedience to said maxim would produce a world worth living in. Both ethical formulas implicitly demote compassion from the status of the unwilled and chaotic basis of all morality, as Schopenhauer construed it, to an instrumentally rational means to the collective end of making everyone better off in the long run.

Towards an ethics writ large 13

In one way or another, therefore, conventional philosophical thought, if not common understanding, has construed ethicality as reason's willing acquiescence in a rationally justified (and collectively imposed and enforced) system of rules and customs designed to constrain the natural selfishness of the individual by threatening social disapproval and offering social rewards. But what reason understands itself to be bidding us to do always takes the form of a message or command that must be understood to be obeyed: "Do (or don't do) X." And the fact that this message or command must, in each and every case, be understood (somehow or other) before it can be obeyed reveals reason's ethical Achilles heel.

In the end – at the moment of acting or not acting – the real human being to whom a rational ethical command is addressed can only passively "receive" what it keeps *urging* (not telling) him or her to do on each new occasion. For each new occasion is particular, not general, and as H. L. A. Hart observed, "Particular fact-situations do not await us already marked off from each other, and labelled as instances of the general rule, the application of which is in question; nor can the rule itself step forward to claim its own instances" (1961: 123). Here Hart seems to appropriate an insight of Wittgenstein's (cf. Hart, 1961: 249). Just as in Wittgenstein's analysis of rule-following (1953: 201e), it is a clear implication of Hart's truism that the distance between a general rule and what any real Self actually does with it in any particular situation is spanned not by a solid bridge of logic, but rather by the Self's very own breathless temporal leap from here to there.

To be sure, others – even many others – may subsequently praise and reward the actor for his "sound ethical judgment"; or they may criticize him for misapplying the ethical command. But so what? A consensus of opinion about the application of a norm is like the consensus of a herd of sheep all going in the same direction: it is something that happens, a part of history. It can be explained by its causes, such as the socialization in individuals of widely shared (and possibly nasty) prejudices about others, or, as in the case of sheep, a yapping sheepdog. But as Hart's remark suggests, social consensus cannot be explained by the inert linguistic signs that constitute the ethical norm as such.

Phenomenally speaking, the last-minute urgings of reason closely resemble the immediate urgings of compassion. Both come from prerational sources which, in the moment of acting or not acting, are not visible to the actor. How a rational ethical norm is received *nudges* the actor in some direction or other during the existential tick-tock, tick-tock of real time unspooling within (or as) this or that concrete, nonidentical ethical situation. After all will have been said and done interpretatively with the words of the ethical command, the actual way the command is received-and-acted-upon in the moment is neither rational nor irrational. Although it may sound insulting to say this, the insult is not intended: the last-minute urgings of

14 *Towards an ethics writ large*

rational ethics are best described as nonrational because history alone has positioned us to react, *à la* Pavlov's salivating dogs, to the words of the command in the way we just *do* react, rather than in some other way.

In the beginning was the deed

The nonrational phenomenon of linguistic reception found its first and most potent expression with the publication of Goethe's tragic play *Faust Part One* in 1808. The eponymous hero of that play famously managed to distill an ocean full of philosophical verbiage about the obvious yet uncanny contrast between words and deeds into a mighty droplet of poetic truth.

Doctor Faust, having learned everything the universities of the world had to teach, decided to study the language of the scriptures, ancient Greek, in order to, as Emily Warner puts it, "translate into his native German the truths the prophets knew" (1997: 123). He got stuck, however, trying to translate the original first line of the Christian Bible's fourth gospel, John 1:1: *En archē ēn ho logos*. The learned Faust first considered the traditional German language translation, *Im Anfang war das Wort* ("In the beginning was the Word"), only to think to himself, "To set so high a value on a 'word' is impossible: I must translate it some other way." Trying out, but then rejecting, two other plausible terms for what there might have been in the beginning – *Sinn* ("meaning") and *Kraft* ("force") – Faust suddenly saw the right answer. The Spirit (*der Geist*), he said, had moved him to translate this canonical biblical passage this way, and this way only: *Im Anfang war die Tat!* ("In the beginning was the *deed*!") (Goethe, 1964: 185).

Faust's final choice of the word "deed" is surely a more accurate translation of what there is or was in the beginning than any of the other alternatives he considered. Words – or if you will, language – must first be thought, spoken, or written down in order to exist at all, let alone produce any effects. To reach this conclusion, one need only submit to receiving (irony intended) a little nudge from the principle of sufficient reason – *nihil est sine ratione*, as Leibniz first expressed it (1934: 8) – a so-called law of logic which stipulates, among other things, that nothing can exist without a sufficient cause or ground for its existing. Thus, if it is true that God's *logos* (Greek for "word," but also "reason" and "plan") successfully summoned the universe into being in the distant past, then the *deed* of his thinking and/or speaking it had to have come first. One suspects that this line of reasoning, or something close to it, explains why Faust translated *logos* as "deed" instead of "word."

The attempt to deduce the world in words from yet another word resembles, as Adorno puts it, "the behavior of someone who would like to usurp power instead of resisting it" (2005: 88). Thus, there is a certain amount of irony in Faust's use of the *word* "deed" to suggest that deeds always come

Towards an ethics writ large   15

before words. Nevertheless, what remains in reality during its description is precisely what is not described: the act of describing itself. One likes to think that Goethe, at least, knew full well that Faust's use of the word "deed" in this context is a gesture, not a description. On this reading, the inequality "deed ≠ word" is not a *said* that expresses a metaphysical truth – it is a *saying*. To write or speak such a thing out loud *deeds* the distinction between words and deeds into being (right now!) by means of what the philosophy of language calls a speech act. The act of saying "In the beginning was the deed" literally makes the saying of it so.

Such an act of saying indicates something about the actor's ethical disposition. It indicates, among other things, that his conscience is probably not going to be satisfied by what others would call the correct "content" of an ethical expression. But what about the received content of his own translation? Ethics and theology aside, what Faust believes holds true for God – deeds precede words – must in any case hold true for human beings, who, after all, are not gods capable of performing miracles. To be sure, it is possible that some or many Christians believe that God is mighty enough to change form, *à la* Zeus, and become an inanimate word-entity that somehow remains animate enough to do things all on its own. That, at least, is one possible reading of John 1:1, which in the Bible's King James version says, in its entirety, "In the beginning was the Word, and the Word was with God, and *the Word was God*" (emphasis added).

But of course human beings have never been able to make their words grow little feet and walk around. Nor have their words ever grown little arms and hands that could, without *any* human help, reach out and touch someone on their own, for good or for ill. This plain-as-vanilla empirical observation explains why a comment on Kant's Categorical Imperative once made by the French poet and editor Charles Péguy only *seems* paradoxical: "Kantian ethics has clean hands but, in a manner of speaking, actually no hands" (Rrenban, 2004: 210).

All human acts of thinking, speaking, and writing words – as well as the mental representations called "ideas" or "concepts" – just like all human acts of understanding, hearing, and reading these things, must themselves always first be set into motion by deeds, not words. What is more, if we accept Leibniz's doctrine of continuous creation to explain why something that was once created can continue to exist through time (1934: 11), then it would not be enough for God (and *a fortiori* human beings) to deed words into being just once; God (and humans) would have to ceaselessly keep on deeding them into being what they are during every moment they persist in reality. Unread books and unseen linguistic signs (i.e. the material embodiments of language) may indeed passively *exist* in libraries, thanks to the ongoing labor of librarians, who probably glance at them every now and then. But eternally unread and unremembered *language* has even less claim

16 *Towards an ethics writ large*

to existence than does the sound made by the proverbial tree that falls in a forest when no one is around to hear it.

Linguistic beginnings that remain forevermore unbegun again are like the score of a song that, once written and put in a drawer, will never in fact be sung or heard. To believe otherwise – to believe that ideas somehow "exist" even if no one ever thinks or talks about them – is a form of magical thinking. Platonism is like this, as is the belief that words (or sentences) have entities called "meanings" attached to them which objectively determine their correct applications in advance of their usage. Wittgenstein cleverly labeled this way of thinking the *Bedeutungskörper* ("meaning-body") theory of language (1978: 54), according to which "meaning is the object for which a word stands" (1953: 2e), and he took great delight in demonstrating, over and over again, the theory's inability to explain how language is actually used by human beings.

But – and this is an important caveat – one need not become a Wittgensteinian to see that reason's usual insistence that its ethical norms have objectively correct, sign-independent meanings (whether Platonic, intended, consensusbased, or otherwise) in advance of their actual applications requires the same kind of faith in the unseen that religion inspires in believers.

This insight leads us into the revolving door of another profoundly true tautology: the fate of the present moment, just like that of every other present moment, is sealed by deeds, and never, ever, by unen*acted* words or ideas. So, too, are the ethical fates of Self and Other sealed only by deeds.

The concept *deeds*, by the way, also includes the kind of deed that we sometimes classify privatively as an inaction or omission. Strictly speaking, reality contains no such thing as an inaction or omission; it only contains, or rather manifests, different ways of acting, such as lying down and snoozing instead of trying to help your neighbor out of a difficulty. "A man need not, it is true, do this or that act, – the term *act* implies a choice," said Oliver Wendell Holmes, "but he must act somehow" (1963: 77). It is ontologically impossible for living human beings not to act in *some* way or other, even if this is only to close their eyes to the spectacle of another's suffering so as to get on with their ordinary lives.

Thus, not acting to address a perceived injustice that is within our power to remedy can always be interpreted as acting in a way that allows it to go on. It is true the law recognizes in most (but not all!) cases that killing someone is not the same as letting them die. But the very fact that the legal system holds some "inactions" to be just as culpable as "actions" (see Tarasoff, 1976) shows that the distinction between these concepts is established by our conventions, and not by the physics or metaphysics of acting as such.

If both reason and compassion must consummate themselves in deeds to produce any ethically significant consequences, then this fact alone makes them look existentially alike, not categorically different. It is a simple

Towards an ethics writ large 17

phenomenological observation that reason's loquacious ethical *telling* can and does pass into mute *urging*, in the form of the pre- or post-rational inner feeling that ethics should be based on the "meaning" of what reason commands, as in Kant's philosophy. It is also a simple phenomenological observation that compassion's ethical *urging* can and often does pass into a loquacious *telling*, as in Schopenhauer's vigorously argued doctrine that ethics is and should be based on compassion (2005). Holding both observations together in one's mind can be disquieting, to say the least. It makes the choice between reason and compassion in ethics, if there is such a choice, look . . . unmoored.

To feel unmoored can be disquieting indeed. Nevertheless, underlying every sentence in this book is the conviction that reason's truest *immorality* consists in its rendering immediate and automatic obedience to its own certainties, whatever these may be.

René Descartes, whose principle of *cogito ergo sum* ("I think, therefore I am") identifies truth with absolute self-certainty, drew a subtle and important distinction between knowing that something exists and grasping it in thought. In a letter to his friend Marin Mersenne, the French polymath and Minim friar, he wrote that it is possible to know something without fully grasping it, "just as we can touch a mountain but not put our arms around it. To grasp something is to embrace it in one's thought; to know something, it suffices to touch it with one's thought" (1984: II, 32 n.1). The metaphors of grasping and touching correspond, in turn, to the epistemological categories of mastery and acquaintanceship. Grasping/mastery produces the feeling that one has completely demystified and internalized what something is, inside and out; touching/acquaintanceship, in contrast, is the state of simply being aware that something nameable exists without also feeling that one has already mastered how to deal with it.

According to Descartes's *Third Meditation*, one of the things that knowledge can touch without grasping is the "nature of the infinite" (1984: II, 32). Whether it be called God or something else, the infinite in this sense is not something that is endlessly long or large, or something that takes a really, really long time to grasp. Rather, the infinite is something whose essential indeterminacy leaves it ungraspable in principle. Or better still, the nameable but ungraspable infinite is something the Self can choose to treat as open, not closed – as experienceable afresh on each new occasion, rather than as just another familiar, manageable iteration of the same. To choose openness over closedness in relating to something else, such as another human being, is to choose indeterminacy over determinacy, spontaneity over routinization, an ethics of compassionate reason over an ethics of reasonable compassion, the rationality of autocritique over the rationality of correct judgment.

The importance of the Cartesian distinction between merely knowing (touching-in-thought) *that* a thing is and fully grasping (embracing-in-thought) *what* it is cannot be overstated. The nature of the infinite is not

18   *Towards an ethics writ large*

some deep mystery waiting to be unraveled by reason. Rather, it represents reason's *choice* not to attempt to standardize that unraveling in advance, and instead to consider each particular instance of unravelling as potentially unique – a tub standing on its own bottom.

Emmanuel Levinas, perhaps the twentieth century's most original philosopher of ethicality, characterized the relation that binds Self to Other "the idea of the infinite" (1996: 19). One gets the impression that Levinas himself believed that this characterization was compelled by the phenomenological facts of the case, rather than by his own choice – an inchoate ethical choice, no less – to think and talk about the ethical relationship in this way. But of course, thinkers not only can choose to describe *what* something is, they also can choose, implicitly or explicitly, *how* to describe it. Following in the footsteps of Descartes and Levinas, this book will choose to approach the original relationship between Self and Other as infinite in the precise sense just discussed, namely, as mysteriously left open in each case, rather than as closed in advance by a pre-commitment to compressing it into some theoretically relevant conceptual determination.

The Cartesian/Levinasian thesis advanced here is that knowledge, the result of reason's acquiescence to its own certainties, can touch-and-name, but cannot grasp-and-master, the infinite fullness of the Self/Other relationship. Yet this original relationship's infinitude means that it is also originating. Seen from a point of view that we will call the "ethical present," the infinite relationship between Self and Other does not just establish the jurisdiction of ethicality as it is conventionally understood, namely, as a matter (or battle) of *words* that reason can bat around at relative leisure, either before or after the fact, like shuttlecocks in a game of badminton.

Instead, underlying the idea of the ethical present is what the poet Anne Carson has called the possibility of "unexhausted time" – a time without prior measure or equivalence as it is being lived (1999: VIII). The original Self/Other relationship in unexhausted time *consummates* ethics ontologically in deeds, as Goethe's Faust might have put it. Unfortunately, the problem with deeds is that they can have morally troublesome causes and conditions that are not fully accessible to the gaze of practical reason during their proper moment, i.e. before they become exhausted "occurrences" in a past that cannot be relived, but only remembered or forgotten.

Beginning at the ending

Hegel's famous (or notorious) dictum, in *Philosophy of Right*, that "the rational is real and the real is rational" manages to distill reason's interpretation of the relationship between Self and Other to its essence (1967: 10). Rational ethics, or ethics writ small, imagines that in principle, if not

Towards an ethics writ large 19

always in fact, reality is like a perfect number. A perfect number (say, 6) is not only divisible without remainder, but also equal to the aliquot sum of all its proper divisors (1 + 2 + 3). Analogously, for rational ethics reality is equivalent to the sum of all its true conceptual determinations.

Seen from the point of view of an ethics writ large, however, reality looks more like a transcendental number, say π. The decimal expansion of the number π not only goes on and on forever, the number also cannot occur as the root of a polynomial equation with rational coefficients. No ethical theory, however complete, can enter into a π-like reality without leaving a remainder that reason cannot acknowledge. Unlike mathematics, though, rational ethics cannot even acknowledge the existence of a remainder *in theory* without risking the loss of its monopoly over the right to say what is right and wrong, true and false, relevant and irrelevant.

An ethics writ large lets an ethics writ small be seen in its proper perspective. If, as Hegel also said, *speculative reason* believes "The True is the whole" (1977: 11), then reality as it is always being lived gives *critical reason* plenty of evidence to believe that the very concept of "ethical truth" itself needs deflating. It needs to be deflated, not discarded. Not only will people always have opinions about what is right and wrong, but also their having at least some preliminary moral reaction to events – some moral intuition, expressed or unexpressed – seems essential if ethics writ large, as this book conceives it, is to have a beginning. If speculative and practical reason take the true to be the whole on any given occasion, then critical reason must stand ready to take the proposition "The whole is the false" (Adorno, 2005: 50) as true on every occasion.

In these pages we will seek the deflationary standpoint of an ethics writ large. Looking out from there at what people do to, and for, one another every day, it becomes possible to notice the fact that even the most masterful ethical ratiocination, once it has managed to squeeze a particular relationship between Self and Other into the prose of a helpful conclusion – "right" or "not right," "duty" or "no duty," etc. – always leaves an unmentioned yet ethically troubling remainder. If the denominator is reason, then the numerator is reality itself, including especially the reality of unacknowledged human suffering. An ethics writ large realizes that no hoped-for ethical content, universal or particular, can be communicated without some form given to it by language. But it also knows that with form, or rather *in* it, there is a sense – an ethically troubling sense – in which language always dissembles the infinite particular that reason aspires to notice, manage, and control.

The modern hard sciences know this already, which is why their methodological principle is not truth, but verisimilitude – not certainty, but probability – not eternal correspondence between theoretical statements and reality, but falsifiability (Popper, 1963). When it comes to moonshots and

20 Towards an ethics writ large

medicine, reason considers the inevitable mismatch between the universal and the particular to be a necessary evil – at worst, a hopefully manageable cost of the scientific process. But ethics is different. There, the dissembling performed by universal ethical categories feeds the desire to control and manage the particular by manufacturing a guilt-relieving feeling of certainty. In this process, any uncertainty that once came from not knowing the particular well enough is gradually (and then all at once) replaced by the feeling that everything of importance about the particular is now completely contained in a universal that leaves behind no worrisome remainder.

But of course, there always is an unassimilated remainder of reality left behind after reason has had its say, and whether this remainder is worrisome or not is a distinctly ethical question that cannot in principle be answered or disposed of by yet another universal. And the reason that this is so can be stated in the form of yet another profoundly true tautology: once reason has finally fallen mute before the deed, as it always must, it can have nothing more to say about the situation at hand. To be sure, reason's favorite put-down, "That's irrelevant," can cow naysayers (e.g. trembling first-year law students) into shutting up. But apart from the latent anti-intellectualism of this move, no amount of rhetorical aggression of this sort can ever extirpate the irrelevant from reality itself. Nor can "That's irrelevant" compel those who brought up the unassimilated remainder in the first place to cease fretting about what reason refuses to acknowledge. Instrumental reason can only attempt to train them, *à la* Pavlov's dogs, to put away childish things, to cease fretting, and to start acquiring what Anton Chekhov called, sarcastically but accurately, "a professional relation to other men's sufferings" (2003: 56).

It is not as if rational ethical theories are completely unfamiliar with the problem of unacknowledged remainders. Thus, for example, Kant's deontological ethics reproaches utilitarianism for wanting to let one person die just to save an entire people from annihilation, on the ground that "if justice goes, there is no longer any value in human being's living on the earth" (1996: 473). Whereas Bentham's utilitarianism reproaches deontological ethics for wanting to make some people suffer even if no good will come of it, thereby "cruelly" increasing the evil of human suffering "to no purpose" (1939: 845). Charmed by its own brilliance, certain of its own rightness, each theory imputes the invisibility of certain ethically troubling remainders to the mote in the eye of the *other* theory (cf. Matthew 7:3); neither theory considers the fact that there is a beam in its own eye which makes different ethically troubling remainders invisible to *it*. Neither theory – indeed no theory of ethics based on reason alone – has the wherewithal to admit that the existence of the remainder poses a universal ethical problem that can only be solved by each individual Self as it lives out, and enacts, the ethical present.

Towards an ethics writ large 21

Bernard Williams's 1973 paper *Ethical Consistency* has already drawn much needed attention to this feature of rational, coherence-based theories such as Kant's and Bentham's by introducing the concept of the "moral remainder" in ethical decision-making. The moral remainder, for Williams, is a function of value pluralism: the idea that "value-conflict is not necessarily pathological at all, but something necessarily involved in human values" (1981: 72). Value pluralism, he contends, implies the possibility of explicitly conflicting values each of which is entitled to some kind of moral recognition even if the ethical agent's actual decision in the moment can only honor one of them. Thinkers such as Kant and Bentham, according to Williams, "falsely project the logic of theoretical reason onto such conflicts, leading to the categorical denial of the conflict as a genuine one and, relatedly, to the denial of the normative bearing of the losing claim" (van Domselaar, 2020: 3). Hence they inappropriately "eliminate from the scene the ought that is not acted upon" (Williams, 1973: 175).

Williams's theory imagines that the abstractions we call "values" only sometimes generate moral remainders in ethical decision-making in cases where someone must win and someone else must lose. For him, the distinctly *moral* dimension of the loser's situation after the ethical agent makes an all-things-considered correct ethical decision is a product of its being grounded in a value that is entitled to respect even if it is not entitled to prevail. Adorno's theory of the remainder is different, for it holds that there is *always* something morally troubling about the attempt to reduce present reality to its conceptual content. The remainder, for Williams, is troublesome because its moral status is determined solely by the application of a concept – a value – that subsumes the loser's case but that does not let him prevail. In contrast, for Adorno, as for this book's notion of an ethics writ large, the remainder is utterly nonconceptual in principle. Its moral status is a function of "the untruth of identity, the fact that the concept does not exhaust the thing conceived" (Adorno, 1973: 5).

Adorno had it right. The self-criticism of reason is indeed its truest morality because this is the only way that an ethically conscientious Self can realize that reason always arrives too late, and compassion too early, to grasp the fullness of the ethical relationship without gainsaying it. Before the deed, an ethics writ small is all about paying attention to and controlling what *will be* the path taken. After the deed, it is all about exonerating or assigning blame on account of the path that *was* taken, or, as in Williams, allowing the ethical agent's feeling of regret to possibly generate acts of mitigation or atonement on account of the harm caused by the path that was not followed (see van Domselaar, 2020: 11). An ethics writ large, on the other hand, comes from critical reason's admission to itself that practical reason – the reason of categorical intuition – is *always* complicit in unethicality no matter how

22 *Towards an ethics writ large*

hard it tries to excuse itself for what, looking forward, it is about to do, or for what, looking backward, it will have done.

There is such a thing as ethics writ large, and it begins where ethics writ small ends.

Notes

1 From the Latin noun *virtus* (merit or moral perfection), from *vir* (man) (wouldn't you know it).
2 From the Greek prefix *deont-* (being necessary) and suffix *-logia* (the study of).
3 From the Greek noun *telos* (purpose or end) and suffix *-logia* (the study of).
4 Ordinary language sometimes distinguishes *ethicality* from *morality*, even though both are about what is right and wrong for individuals to do. Sometimes people say that "ethics" imposes external rules and principles on individuals (e.g. ethics codes) and "morals" consist in the individual's internal normative rules and principles (if any). However, "most ethicists (that is, philosophers who study ethics) consider the terms interchangeable" (Grannan, 2020), and this book will do the same.
5 *First formulation of Kant's Categorical Imperative*: "Act only in accordance with that maxim through which you can at the same time will that it become a general law"; *second formulation*: "Act as if the maxim of your action were to become by your will a universal law of nature" (1996: 73); *third formulation*: "So act that you can use humanity, whether in your own person or in the person of any other, always at the same time as an end, and never merely as a means" (1996: 80); *fourth formulation*: "The above three ways of representing the principle of morality are at bottom only so many formulae of the very same law, and any one of them of itself unites the other two in it" (1996: 85).
6 From the Greek noun *noumenon* (something conceived), from the verb *noein* (to conceive or apprehend).
7 From the Greek noun *phainomenon* (thing appearing to view), from the verb *phainein* (to show).
8 An *internal relation* is "an interpropositional relation that relates the situations described in the propositions by their communicative usage as opposed to relating the situations described by the propositions"; an *external relation* as "an inter-propositional relation which relates the situations described in the propositions by experiential, extralinguistic reality as opposed to relating them by the solely communicative usage of propositions" (Halliday & Hasan, 1976: 239–41).
9 "[G]ood men will all display mercy and gentleness, but pity [*misericodrdia*] they will avoid; for it is the failing of a weak nature that succumbs to the sight of others' ills" (Seneca, 1928: 439).
10 "Pity [*Commiseratio*] in a man who lives according to the guidance of reason is in itself evil and unprofitable" (Spinoza, 1955: 224).
11 "Even this feeling of compassion and tender sympathy, if it precedes consideration of what is duty and becomes the determining ground [of action], is itself burdensome to right-thinking persons, brings their considered maxims into confusion, and produces the wish to be freed from them and subject to lawgiving reason alone" (Kant, 1996: 235).

2 From *ethōs* to ethics

Custom [*Nomos*] is lord of everything,/Of mortals and immortals king./
High violence it justifies,/With hand uplifted plundering.

Pindar (1938: 296)

If a person does not become what he understands, he does not really understand it.

Søren Kierkegaard (1993: 126)

From custom to character to duty

According to conventional understanding, legal duties and ethical duties are supposed to belong to different categories of obligation, at least in societies with non-theocratic forms of government. Legal duties refer to one's obligations to the state or to private rights-holders and are enforced by the threat of coercive governmental sanctions, such as imprisonment, fines, injunctions, and damage awards, whereas ethical duties refer to a variety of legally unenforceable moral obligations owed by individuals to other individuals, if not society as a whole. The category of ethics writ small in this way typically includes such anodyne obligations as remaining loyal to one's friends, telling the truth, showing respect for others, promise-keeping, and so forth.

Everyone knows, of course, that legal and ethical duties sometimes overlap – some promises are legally enforceable, for example, just as some lies can create legal liability. Absent any overlap with the law, however, it is generally supposed that purely ethical duties derive from nongovernmental principles whose origin might be religious or secular, but whose worldly enforcement, if any, can only come from two possible sources: (1) the actor's own conscience prodding him or her to do the right thing, and/or (2) the actor's self-regarding fear of negative social or economic consequences should others find out about his or her behavior and disapprove of it as unethical.

24   *From* ethōs *to ethics*

Actually, though, even the most comprehensive catalogue of ethical duties imposed on individuals by even the most reasonable-looking moral norms would not account for all of the historical and contemporary usages of the concept of ethicality. One might say that ethics, like the poet Walt Whitman, is large and contains multitudes (1950: 74). Or that ethics, which in all cases seems to concern only the individual Self's moral relationship (as a *Me-Myself*) to the Other, also contains, as does the law, the collective *We-Ourselves* (the insider's point of view) and *They-Themselves* (the outsider's point of view) of history in the form of social custom, culture, and politics.

The word *ethics* itself comes from the Greek noun *ethōs*. In its plural form (*ethea*), the term first made its appearance in Western literature in the *Iliad* (6.511), where Homer used it to denote the customary place or habitat of horses (*ethea ippon*). Later on, the poet Hesiod and the historian Herodotus would employ the word *ethōs* and its cognates to designate the customs or habits of human social groups (Brown, 1999: 10–11 n.43). An echo of this descriptive use of *ethōs* can still be heard today whenever historians or sociologists refer to the "ethos" of a given era or society without making any explicit moral judgments about its goodness or badness. Ideally, to describe a society's ethos in this sense means to give an account of the way most people in that society ordinarily do behave, not how they should behave. The English word "mores" (from the plural of the Latin noun *mos*, for custom or habit) has a similar meaning.

If horses and human societies can have their own *ethea*, then why not individual human beings? A fragment attributed to the pre-Socratic philosopher Heraclitus shows that at some point in the history of Western thought the word *ethōs* began to be applied to individuals: *Ethōs anthropoi daimōn* ("A person's character is his fate") (1987: 69). This aphorism uses *ethōs* to refer to the state of a particular individual's habitual way of being – a person's "character,"[1] as Heraclitus's translator (and we) have come to call it – although still in a purely descriptive sense of the word. Saying that a person's *ethōs* is his fate means that everyone eventually exhibits some habitual way of thinking, speaking, and acting that makes them who they are and determines (or at least co-determines) how they will act, whether for good or ill. The English word *character* can also be used descriptively in this way, as in Charlie Chaplin's famous *bon mot*, "A man's true character comes out when he's drunk." On this reading of *ethōs*, one's character stands in relation to one's actions as a cause does to its effects, or more broadly, as the present does to the future.

The modern professional codes noted at the beginning of Chapter 1 are fundamentally different, as are the principles and obligations at stake in most conventional discussions of moral philosophy. They explicitly present themselves as normative statements rather than as mere lexicons for use in making

From ethōs *to ethics*   25

value-neutral descriptions. A normative statement compares a verbal indication or description of some reality that exists, existed, or will exist (let's call this an *Is*) against some verbal standard for what it should be or should have been (let's call this an *Ought*). The intellectual great-great-grandparents of ethical normativity in this sense were Socrates, Plato, and especially Aristotle, who used the term *ethikos*, the adjectival cognate of *ethōs*, to refer to the quality, and not just the facticity, of a given person's character. Good character, said Aristotle, "is a state concerned with choice, lying in a mean relative to us, this being determined by reason and in the way in which the man of practical wisdom would determine it" (1106^{b}36–1107^{a}1–3).

Aristotle did not believe that a person's character is simply a given fact that can only be observed and described in a dispassionate, ho-hum sort of way, *à la* the customs and habits of horses or societies. Nor did he hold that people are born with unchangeable characters that predetermine their fates in life. Rather, Aristotle thought that a person's character is something that can and should be improved and maintained through education (*paideia*) and, more importantly, through conscientious care and improvement of the self (*epimeleia heautou*). Thus, by the third century BCE the Greek word for "ethics," originally employed as a noun to describe the customary behavior of equines (an *Is*), then social custom (another *Is*), and then an individual's extant character (yet another *Is*), had at last been transformed into a procedure for evaluating one's presently existing character (an *Is*) according to some criterion for having a good character (an *Ought*). In sum, a person's character (*ethōs*) had metamorphosed into something that demanded measurement – by the person himself and by others – against the then-prevailing social ideal of human virtue (*aretē*).

For Aristotle and most of his Greek contemporaries the normative ideal at which human virtue aimed was living well (*eu zēn*), which meant living in such a way as to produce a flourishing human life (*eudaimonia*, sometimes misleadingly translated as "happiness"). The hard work of developing and maintaining a virtuous character (*ēthikē aretē*) over a lifetime became, for them, a universal *Ought*, albeit one that might yield different results for different sorts of men according to their circumstances. (Not for women, though, whose *ethea* were limited by men to matters of hearth and home.) In someone who possesses a virtuous character, said Aristotle, reason and emotion – the rational and the nonrational – speak with "the same voice" (*homophōnei*) (1102^{b}28). The normative ideal of his ethical system therefore logically excluded the possibility of conflict between reason and compassion in the mind of the virtuous individual.

Strange as it may sound to modern ears, Aristotelian virtue ethics did not furnish a rule or procedure for deciding whether a particular action is or is not ethically valid. The relevant entity to be compared with the Greek ideal

26   *From* ethōs *to ethics*

of personal virtue was not the actor's ethically questionable *action* – it was the actor's ethically questionable *character*. To put it anachronistically, it is as if Aristotle sought to hardwire a person's character to his actions in such a way as to make a dispositive difference, both factually and morally, whether the character in question was vicious or virtuous. "To play the coward or act unjustly consists not in doing these [specific bad] things, except incidentally," he said, "but in doing them as the result of a certain state of character" (1137ª20–25). Although he recognized that there is a sense in which particular actions can be right or wrong regardless of who commits them, he also believed that in thinking about ethics it is far more important to understand that good actions proceed naturally from someone who possesses a virtuous character, and conversely, that bad actions tend to proceed naturally from someone whose character is vicious, or at least insufficiently virtuous.

In the heyday of Stoicism – during the Hellenistic period and the ascendancy of the Roman Empire – ethics was still seen as the practice of attaining and maintaining a virtuous character, but now with an added twist. If Aristotle had cut the Gordian knot of complex moral problems with the notion of having a virtuous character, then Stoicism wagered everything it had on the use of reason to untie the knot, strand by strand, case by case. In particular, the Stoic doctrine of natural attachment to what is appropriate (*oikeiōsis*) insisted that it is possible to objectively order each individual choice as good or bad by undertaking a rational analysis of that course of action most in accordance with nature (see Baltzly, 2018). Stoicism thus set the stage for the ethical criticism of particular actions as such, considered apart from the general state of the actor's character.

Sacrificing much nuance in the interest of brevity, it would be fair to say that eventually Christianity, and ultimately secular philosophy, attempted to enclose the word *ethics* inside a semantic circle by interpreting it as the obligatory task of conforming one's actions, rather than one's character, to certain objective standards established by rational moral rules and principles. Ethics viewed as an ongoing diachronic imperative to develop, improve, and maintain the virtuousness of one's character eventually morphed into what we have today: ethics viewed as an on-again, off-again synchronic imperative to follow the moral norm that is most appropriate to each new situation as it arises.

Like an eternal sleepwalker being guided hither and yon by successive caretakers, the task of being ethical gradually lost touch with the cultivation of good character and drifted into the realm of case-by-case practical reasoning. Where once the true origin of ethics was seen to consist in the routinization of an individual's good moral character, now it became the individual's capacity to correctly understand statements of binding ethical norms that must be found or inferred from authoritative sources. The

From ethōs *to ethics* 27

Christian Bible, for example, or the voice of Aquinas's "right reason" (*recta ratio*) (1952: 633), or Kant's Categorical Imperative (1996: 73). Like an echo in an otherwise noisy room of a sound made long ago, the modern rediscovery of "virtue ethics" in certain quarters of moral philosophy is the exception that proves the rule (irony intended) that most people think of ethics as a rule-governed enterprise.

The codependency of *Is* and *Ought* as an elective affinity

The difference between *ethōs* in its original sense and *ethics* in its modern sense corresponds to the contrast between the descriptive and the normative. The latter is not just a grammatical distinction, like the difference between the active voice and the passive voice. Nor is it semantic only, like the different meanings of the words "dog" and "cat." It also reflects an almost metaphysical *opposition* in conventional ethical discourse: *Is* versus *Ought*. Despite its taken-for-granted usage in ordinary language and in scholarly papers, however, the opposition between *Is* and *Ought* should never be viewed as absolute, especially not here.

This book's idea of an ethics writ large depends almost entirely on the ability to distinguish between *thing-language*, seen as an object, and the *reception of language*, seen as an event. The concept of "thing-language" interprets language as the perduring unity of something that is *said*: it imagines that otherwise free and independent subjects use a material object (a linguistic sign, X) that seems to point away from itself to something else (its meaning, Y). The concept of "reception of language," on the other hand, interprets language as an ephemeral *saying*: it imagines the use of language as a unique and holistic happening of a subject-and-object messily mushed together in a particular ethical present.

The juxtaposition of language seen as a *being* and language seen as *being received* brings out the fact that the application of any ethical norm is always preceded and determined – or at least urged – by what lies outside the four corners of the norm viewed as a symbolic object. A norm's application depends, in short, on the way that history in the largest sense of the word – the big *Is* of culture, custom, Wittgenstein's "language-games," etc. – has always already positioned the actor to receive-and-act-upon the norm's concrete representations in daily life. It's not just *what* a norm says, in general, that is historically contingent, but also *how* the norm's expression affects each one of us, in particular, in the ethical present of each new occasion.

What is the ethical present? The sixth-century Roman philosopher Boethius famously observed that the now that passes produces the idea of tripartite time (past, present, and future), but "the now that remains produces eternity" (*nunc stans facit aeternitatum*) (2012: 168 n.46). The ethical present can be thought of, perhaps oxymoronically, as a finite form of

28   *From* ethōs *to ethics*

eternity. Finite because no Self lives forever. Eternal because past and future are not hermetically separate in the ethical present. Rather, they are present *in* the now that remains – Boethius's *nunc stans* – as each particular Self, so long as it is alive, keeps on making and remaking – always right now – the future on the basis of the past.

There are many ways of trying to describe what Boethius called the *nunc stans*, the now that remains. For example, Edmund Husserl's phenomenology of internal time consciousness labels the immediate copresence of the past in the now "retention" and the immediate copresence of the future in the very same now "protension" (1990: 88–89). Another example: Martin Heidegger's phenomenological critique of traditional ontology's "inauthentic" (*uneigentlich*) tripartite division of time holds that the "has been" (*Vergangenheit*) of the past actually arises from our always already "being futural" (*Zukünftigsein*) in the now (1962: 373–75). Rather than getting lost in the weeds of intellectual history and exegetical controversy, however, let's just say that for our purposes the ethical present is what frames the particular where and when of every real encounter between a Me and a You, a Him and a Her, or more broadly still, Self and Other.

Among other things, the factual claim (*Is*) being asserted here is that the activity of "correctly" following any norm (ethical, legal, religious, etc.) in the ethical present is like a person's character in its earliest Greek sense: an effect, *right now*, of many causes, many (or most) of which elude the actor's conscious awareness. Most critical social theories accept or presuppose the truth of this claim as their most important methodological principle. Adorno conveniently summarized it this way: "knowledge comes to us through a network of prejudices, opinions, innervations, self-corrections, presuppositions and exaggerations, in short through the dense, firmly-founded but by no means uniformly transparent medium of experience" (2005: 80). A case in point is the difference between conscious racial prejudice seen as this or that person's uniquely subjective failing (the "bad apple" theory) and racism seen as an objective social-historical milieu framing the countless ways that relationships and outcomes are routinely constituted, over and over again, in daily life even in the absence of someone's conscious racial prejudice ("institutional racism").

The ethical claim (*Ought*) being recommended here is that this very fact should worry us, should give us pause. The sadism latent in everyone, as Adorno puts it, unerringly divines the weakness latent in everyone, including even the diviner's own Self (2005: 163). The hope for a better world constructed on the basis of institutional changes in politics and law tends to interpret the weakness of others as a kind of masochism – a latent desire on the part of everyone else for correction, whether or not they presently know it. Anyone who realizes this, and who remains unable or unwilling to shut

From ethōs *to ethics* 29

their eyes to the spectacle of suffering that is everywhere on display in the world today, cannot fail to see the violence latent, and often patent, in every form of human organization. Hence, they cannot fail to ask this question: Whom do we crush underfoot in today's now in the name of a political and legal morality that has been informed by a certain knowledge that in tomorrow's now we will regret ever having called "knowledge"?

To be very clear, the concept "actual application of an ethical norm" is an instance of what Chapter 1 called "the deed," *à la* Goethe's Faust. In particular, it refers to the Self's doing something in the ethical present – anything, really – that inflicts, tolerates, or otherwise fails to relieve the avoidable suffering of the Other while at the same time consciously believing that it is merely doing its duty on the basis of what the norm "says." It is obvious, for example, that the ethical norm "Thou shalt not steal" (an *Ought*) would be an impenetrable cypher unless the person whom it seems to address first knows or senses – or is otherwise inhabited by – *some* customary social ethos (an *Is*) of what kinds of things are stealable and what sorts of actions count as "stealing" them. Once inculcated and represented in the individual, "in however etiolated a form" (Adorno, 2005: 36–37), glacially malleable social conventions of ethicality usually forget their origin in history and insist on being treated as context-transcending "universal" prohibitions to which people can earnestly appeal in making, or resisting, the sorts of claims they seem to allow.

The dependency of our inner sense of normativity on its social-historical causes – of *Ought* on *Is* – usually fails to emerge as a moral quandary in the consciousness of the typical, well-socialized ethical agent. To be well-socialized consists in generally conforming your behavior to the ways other people around you behave without thinking too much about it, if at all. All men wear hats and all women wear corsets, until they don't. Even anger against the general customs of the majority (Is_1) is generally steered in advance by the counter-customs of one or more angry, if not rebellious, groups (Is_2). "The enraged man," as Adorno puts it, "always appears as the gang-leader of his own self, giving his unconscious the order to pull no punches, his eyes shining with the satisfaction of speaking for the many that he himself is" (2005: 45). Whether the angry individual's deeds are great or ignoble, successes or failures, engines of unjust suffering or augurs of a justice-to-come, they can almost always be traced to some conventional groupthink or other. Which is the only way convention can act: through the individual, or rather, through lots of like-acting individuals.

It follows that we are all sheep – *to one degree or another* – even when we think we are playing the uniquely originating role of a lone wolf. The *Them* and the *Us* lurking inside each and every *Me-Myself* makes us human beings, makes us socially strong or weak, makes us politically and

30   *From* ethōs *to ethics*

economically effective or ineffective: that's the good news (and bad). In his 1953 book *The Captive Mind*, the Polish writer Czeslaw Miloz famously described the social and psychological rewards to the individual of nonresistance to the demand for conformity inside a Stalinist state (1990). But the reduction of stress, and even the tranquility, that can come from "fitting in" with *Us* (and avoiding being identified with *Them*) is not confined to the limiting case of totalitarianism. Ethical blindness in a "bad" police state and ethical blindness in a "good" democratic state are siblings, not strangers.

The bad news (and good) is that *Them* and *Us* are collectively capable of doing monstrous things to the Other that only the individual Self is in a position to resist during the ethical present of this or that particular encounter with this or that particular Other. If empirical confirmation of this unsettling mixture of bad news and good news were ever needed, then a recent essay by the writer Francisco Cantú – a third-generation Mexican American and former agent of the U.S. Border Patrol working in the deserts of the American Southwest to catch undocumented immigrants – goes a long way to provide it:

> When the violence of our institutions is revealed, when their dehumanizing design is laid bare, it can be too daunting to imagine that we might change things. But what I have learned from giving myself over to a structure of power, from living within its grim vision and helping to harm the people and places from which I came, is that even the most basic act of decency can serve as a spark that will lead one back toward humanity, and even the most basic individual interaction has the power to upend the idea of the "other."
>
> (2019: 6)

The collective politics of *Us* versus *Them* can move mountains. But only the intimate ethical politics (so to speak) of each particular *Me-Myself* can hope to save a helpless Other – whatever his or her affiliations may be – from the hurtful effects of the resulting tremors and landslides (see Levinas, 1998: 230).

Of course, there are certain liminal situations in which individual *habit* (Is_1) and social *custom* (Is_2) do not coincide, even in the well-socialized person. One such phenomenon is what Chapter 1 called the nonrational irruption of "senseless kindness," about which more will be said later. Another situation can be illustrated by a well-known cinematic example that will strike a familiar chord in any traveler who has ever felt uncomfortably ignorant about the right way to do things inside a foreign culture.

A white pilot flying over the Kalahari Desert casually tosses an empty bottle of Coca-Cola out the window. Undoubtedly this minor bad act of littering would have been comprehensible as such to the pilot (i.e. as "littering"),

From ethōs *to ethics*   31

at least if he had thought about it. But when Xi, a member of the isolated San tribe of African bushmen, finds the miraculously unbroken bottle on the ground, he has no idea what the mysterious object is, since he had never seen such a thing before. The plot of the 1980 South African film *The Gods Must Be Crazy* unfolds as an extended comedic meditation on the difference between the pilot's and the San tribe's interpretations of the bottle's significance.

The movie's most important lesson for the project of thinking about ethics comes from three interrelated insights. First, the historical antecedents (the *Is*'s) of the pilot's life experiences and those of the San people are *in fact* radically different. Second, this difference *in fact* determines two radically different *Oughts* for how the bottle can and should be treated. To the pilot, the bottle is disposable junk. To Xi and the San's elders, the bottle is a supernaturally cursed thing that causes the tribe so much misfortune that Xi is ordered to remove it past the edge of the world. Third, unless the pilot and the San people somehow become consciously aware of the foregoing differences – unless they are somehow made to confront *the fact* that the bottle's significance (its *Ought*) is a function of the different cultural antecedents of those who handle it rather than something inherent in the bottle as such – they will probably think their own interpretation of the bottle is self-evidently true. The essential ambiguity of the bottle will lie beyond their ken, and therefore beyond their ethical concern.

Seen from the point of view that we have been calling ethics writ large, that sort of cluelessness is or should be a matter of ethical concern. Not because of some abstract theory holding that all human moral sensibility is "in fact" (*Is*) historically and culturally relative, and therefore "anything goes" (*Ought*), but because that very fact, or at least its possibility, is generally invisible to us as actors. And the more ardent our belief is in the absolute rightness of our conduct, the more invisible – and hence unquestionable – is the rightness or wrongness of its origin and its consequences.

So, *Is* implies *Ought* (*Is→Ought*). But it is also the case that *Ought* implies *Is* (*Ought→Is*). *Ought*'s dependency on *Is* from the "subjective" point of view of the ethical actor – who imagines, based on *Is*, that he is merely doing what he ought to do – is matched by *Is*'s dependency on *Ought* from the "objective" point of view of an observer, who imagines, based on *Ought*, that he is merely describing what is the case. Among other things, this is another way of saying that no respectable contemporary historian or sociologist believes that it is possible, or even desirable, to give a completely value-free account of any human phenomenon – to definitively say "how it really was," as Leopold von Ranke, the founder of nineteenth-century German historicism, would have put it (2011: 86). Social science has long known that rendering a completely value-free description of social facts is also beyond our capacity. "There is no absolutely 'objective' scientific

32 *From* ethōs *to ethics*

analysis of culture," said the great German sociologist Max Weber, that is "independent of special and 'one-sided' viewpoints according to which – expressly or tacitly, consciously or unconsciously – they are selected, analyzed and organized for expository purposes" (1949: 72).

Thus, *The Gods Must Be Crazy* should not be narrowly interpreted as just another amusing artistic rendering of the sociological insight that the history of "exotic" social groups, including their routinized systems of value, affects both what members of those groups notice as a fact and how they interpret what they notice. The movie also shows Xi encountering a lovelorn white research biologist, Andrew Steyn, who collects rhinoceros manure and says that rhinos like to stomp out fires. Whence did the character Steyn, a representative of modern Western science, acquire his own sense of what is and what ought to be? The answer is that he acquired it, or rather was imbued with it, from the same sort of source that Xi acquired his.

Modern science's self-image is that of a rigorously nonnormative endeavor that prides itself on finding out what is, whether or not it ought to be. Like Detective Jack Webb in the 1950s television series *Dragnet*, science demands "Just the facts, Ma'am" of any subject matter it investigates. There is at least a strong family resemblance between the scientific attitude and that of Xi and the San people as they try to figure out in the movie what the bottle really "is" before deciding what to do with it. As Weber reminds us, there is no reason why the behaviors of biologists and social scientists, being members of social groups themselves, cannot be made subject to their own methodological principles, namely, *Is→Ought* and *Ought→Is*, which, taken together, can be reduced for the sake of convenience to a single methodological principle: *Is↔Ought*.

Metaphorically speaking the "purely descriptive" net that modern social scientists cast into the waters of social life can also be used by others to catch *them* in the act of throwing it (see, e.g., Husserl, 1970: 23–59). Whatever social scientists might think they should do professionally with a phenomenon such as the San people's relationship with a Coke bottle has the same ultimate origin as what the San people themselves think they should do with the bottle itself. That origin, in a nutshell, is customary ways of knowing and acting (*Is*'s) within the sociolinguistic group or subgroup to which they belong.

It would be difficult to find any serious thinker these days who does not share Weber's opinion about the relation between *Is* and *Ought* in social research. An observer's decisions about what and how to investigate – to research this phenomenon instead of that phenomenon, to look at this kind of evidence and not that kind of evidence, to accept this theory of social ordering as a working hypothesis or some other theory, and so forth – are based on nothing if not the observer's own sense of what is good or valuable

From ethōs *to ethics*   33

to know. Any description of the facts is simultaneously an implied normative warranty that these particular facts are not only worth knowing, but also worth knowing in the particular way that the describer has chosen to collate, assess, and express them. A law-and-economics scholar might describe a given period of legal history in terms of the individual incentives created by then-prevailing legal norms; a Marxist historian might describe the same history in terms of class conflict and ideology; a feminist legal historian might describe it in terms of gender relations; and so forth.

The point is not that one approach is right and the others wrong. It's not even that all approaches are equally right, albeit each in its own way. The point is simply that *Is* and *Ought* stand in a mostly covert relation of codependency that has profound *ethical* implications precisely because we are usually not aware of it. Anyone who chooses to become more-or-less habitually aware of the *Is/Ought* codependency as a general matter also denies herself the right to have a good conscience *vis-à-vis* the Other by virtue of merely "discovering" the objective facts and then "correctly applying" to them some appropriate notion of what ought to be. Once again: social consensus determines correctness, but history determines social consensus.

Historically common social practices such as human sacrifice to appease the gods, slavery, and coverture were once considered *Ought*s that predetermined which otherwise objective facts (*Is*'s) were relevant to their performance. Most people today would probably say these practices were abhorrent because the norms expressing them were wrongheaded and immoral. But of course the *Ought*s underlying such a thing as slavery were not bad merely because of what they *said*. They were bad because of what people actually *did* with them each and every moment to reproduce facts (*Is*'s) that were taken for granted as objectively true. In an ethics writ large, the beginning is always the deed (Goethe's Faust again).

That is why it would be a profound mistake – indeed an ethical evasion – to object to the insight expressed in the formula *Is↔Ought* on the ground that the lesson it teaches can also be made to apply to those who apply it. Ever since the fourth century BCE, when Eubulides invented the Cretan paradox,[2] the clever have known how to embarrass anyone who claims that a statement like *Is↔Ought* expresses an absolute truth. They need only point out that the assertion, if intended as a positivistic description of fact, is hoisted on its own petard, for it clearly says that there can be no such thing as an *Ought*-independent fact.

For present purposes, such a Eubulides-like retort would be too clever by half. The salience of the *Is/Ought* codependency for us lies beyond the jurisdiction of any truth table. Truth in ethics, as history has led us to understand it, is the possession of a Self that has absorbed the Other's situation into itself in the form of a knowledge that is complete and leaves no remainder.

34   *From* ethōs *to ethics*

But an ethics that cares about remainders, as this book conceives them, includes what Adorno calls an attitude of "distanced nearness" (2005: 90) to one's own well-worn epistemological routines. In the context of an ethics writ large, an attitude of distanced nearness would try to counterbalance the eagerness to know with a wary reluctance to let customary ways of knowing automatically determine the outcome of the Self's encounter with the Other.

The conventional distinction in analytic philosophy between views *in* ethics and views *of* ethics is a useful form of intellectual housekeeping, and we do not mean to disparage its utility here (see Lacey, 1986: 66–69). The distinction helps to slice and dice the world of ethical thought along familiar lines, and as such it can be academically fruitful. For example: author A's theory is deontological and author B's theory is teleological (two popular views "in" modern normative ethics). Or author C's ethical theory is merely descriptive and author D's metaethical theory seeks to establish what is universally good and bad, while author E's theory of moral psychology discusses the phenomena of pain and pleasure and author F's theory of moral epistemology asks how we know what is right and wrong (four popular views "of" philosophical ethics). But of course the *in ethics/of ethics* binary classifies ethical theories according to exactly the same dogmatic distinction between *Is* and *Ought* that we have taken pains to deconstruct.

And why have we chosen to deconstruct it? Do we hate all facts and factual statements? No. In the context of the present investigations, at least, the task of recognizing the codependency of *Is* and *Ought* is not just an academic exercise, not just a methodological principle useful for producing tenure-worthy, socially aware scholarship. Choosing to cultivate and maintain an attitude of wariness about the possibly toxic codependency of *Is* and *Ought* is also an ethical deed. It admits to, and thereby recognizes, the ethical importance of what Goethe (1971) and Weber (1976) called an "elective affinity" (*Wahlverstandschaften*) between *Is* and *Ought*. Borrowed from medieval alchemy, the concept of elective affinity as used here refers to a "process through which two cultural forms . . . enter into a relationship of reciprocal attraction and influence, mutual selection, active convergence, and mutual reinforcement" (Löwy, 2004: 6).

If we are all caught in the same historically woven net of apparent objectivity (*Is*) that we throw over events to establish their *Ought*, then this can only mean that we are all morally complicit in sustaining the form of life that we keep on producing. A person's character is his fate indeed, albeit in a sense that is probably much broader than Heraclitus envisioned. For character is in part a byproduct of history, and history contains countless ethically correct colonial administrators, slavecatchers, and wife-beaters who thought they knew exactly what the then-prevailing social customs and norms "told" them to do with the facts as they found them. If the sole criterion of

From ethōs *to ethics*   35

ethicality is what everyone else at the time thinks is right and wrong, then Pindar's poem (quoted in this chapter's epigram) would not only be right, but right absolutely: morality and social consensus would always be the same no matter what bloody horrors their confluence may produce.

The untranslatability of metaphysical statements in ethics

It is undeniable that the distinction between the descriptive and the normative plays an important role in everyday language and the routines of countless social practices, including those involved in law, science, and economic affairs. But to say that a linguistic distinction like *Is* versus *Ought* is a useful means to widely accepted ends – e.g. enforcing legal rights, predicting the behavior of heavenly bodies, and making money – is hardly the same as saying that reality as such is made up of two objective parts: things that are and the shadows, so to speak, of things that should be. *Pace* Plato's theory of eternal forms (*eidoi*), not many sophisticated thinkers these days would argue that the distinction between *Is* and *Ought* – or facts and values – expresses an unassailable, ethically compelling *metaphysical*[3] truth about the nature of reality as such.

"The word 'metaphysics' is notoriously hard to define," according to one leading survey of the field (van Inwagen & Sullivan, 2014). Aristotle famously called the subject matter of metaphysics "first philosophy" (1003[a]22–31) and described it as the study of the necessary – i.e. nonaccidental, non-contingent – elements of "being as being" (1004[a]3). Whatever else it may be, metaphysics tends to deal with certain "big questions" that science is not equipped to answer, questions like "What is the true nature of goodness?" and "Do we have free will?" In legal philosophy, many think the big metaphysical questions include ones such as these: "Are there really correct answers to all (or most) disputed legal questions?"(cf. Dworkin, 1977: 82–90) and "What is the true nature of justice?" (cf. Rawls, 1971: 11–17).

Now, scientific claims, no matter how persuasive and useful they may be, must in principle be falsifiable – i.e. true or false, according to the evidence – whereas metaphysical claims are typically framed in absolute terms. For example, the assertion of the pre-Socratic founder of metaphysics, Parmenides, that what is, is, and "cannot not be," is expressed in such a way that any counterexample you might give to contest it would *eo ipso* be something itself and therefore cannot not be (1984: 55). You might reject this account on aesthetic or religious grounds in favor of some other absolute metaphysical account, such as Heraclitus's that everything is in flux, and therefore nothing (except change itself) ever really "is" (1987: 25). No proffered counterexample can disprove the thesis that everything changes, for

36 *From* ethōs *to ethics*

the very second it comes out of your mouth it is no longer present, and therefore it is different from what it was a moment ago, if only by virtue of its different time index. Hence the plausibility of Heraclitus's statement, "The sun is not only new each day, but forever continuously new" (1987: 13).

But supposing that you did reject Parmenides in favor of Heraclitus, or vice versa, you would not be rejecting the principle of metaphysical absolutism as such. Neither science nor any other form of practical reason is equipped to prove *or* disprove claims like those of Parmenides and Heraclitus, precisely because they are made in such a way as to be irrefutable in principle. Like belief in God, you either cling to them emotionally, or you don't.

Over the centuries, metaphysicians such as Spinoza and Hegel have generally followed the example set by Parmenides by presenting their claims as true absolutely rather than as possibly or contingently true. A statement like "It's raining outside" is meteorologically relevant but metaphysically irrelevant precisely because it could be true *or* false, depending on the weather. But an assertion such as Spinoza's that in nature everything is determined and nothing is contingent (1955: 65) is quite different. Absolute determinism stands ready to refute any proffered counterevidence of contingency by pointing out that whatever phenomenon is relied upon to prove that determinism is false must itself have had a cause.

When it comes to thinking about ethics in relation to law and justice, a particularly important instance of metaphysical absolutism is Hegel's concept of *Sittlichkeit* ("ethical life" or "ethical order") (1967: 319 n.75). According to Hegel, history is essentially the unfolding of the aspects and stages of freedom, albeit a special kind of freedom – one that consummates itself in the ascent of objective Spirit (*Geist*) rather than in the spread of vapid, contentless individual liberty. The concept of *Sittlichkeit* construes the long historical passage from *ethōs* (the *Is* of social custom) to *ethōs* (the *Is* of individual character) to *ethics* (the *Ought* of individual duty) to *Sittlichkeit* (the consolidated *Is/Ought* of the ethical order) as dialectical[4] rather than linear. Among other things, this means that historical progress in ethics is not simply about individuals choosing to replace worse ethical norms with better ones, a movement that Hegel associated with the development of merely subjective "morality" (*die Moralität*). Rather, he saw progress in ethics as an absolutely objective process of Spirit *qua* world history continually striving to replace, and actually replacing, worse normativity *as a whole* with better normativity *as a whole*.

For Hegel, the historical dialectic between individual and collective conceptions of ethicality eventually results in a kind of friendly merger in which the individual's freedom to be bound to the progress of world-Spirit incorporates and transcends all merely political forms of liberation aimed at overcoming peskier, more commonsensical types of bondage. *Sittlichkeit*

From ethōs *to ethics*   37

reaches its apotheosis when each and every fully developed individual's actual ethical character and disposition (an *Is*) corresponds completely to the sum of all fully developed social *Oughts* as these are expressed in terms of law, morality, and custom. Hegel's metaphysical system thus guarantees in advance that the distinction between *Is* and *Ought* will eventually dissolve itself inside a happily unanimous, well-adjusted interpretation of reality – one that leaves behind no messy, unconceived remainders, or at least none that our consciences should acknowledge.

Hence Hegel will say "World history is world justice," as if everything that has ever actually happened was, is, and continues to be absolutely necessary for the supremely just state of affairs called *Sittlichkeit* to finally emerge triumphant (Abelson & Nielsen, 1967: 98). The Hegelian notion of *Aufhebung* (sublation) stipulates that each new stage of history both preserves and transcends what went before – a prospect that filled Adorno, for one, with appalled incredulity:

> Had Hegel's philosophy of history embraced this age [World War II], Hitler's robot-bombs would have found their place beside the early death of Alexander and similar images, as one of the selected empirical facts by which the state of the world-spirit manifests itself directly in symbols. Like Fascism itself, the robots career without subject. Like it they combine utmost technical perfection with total blindness. And like it they arose mortal terror and are wholly futile. "I have seen the world spirit," not on horseback [like Napoleon], but on wings and without a head, and that refutes, at the same stroke, Hegel's philosophy of history.
> (2005: 55)

It is one thing for world history to sublate Hitler's buzz-bombs and death factories into the unity of Spirit's ascent, for these, at least, can be conceptualized to some degree. It is another thing to ignore or suppress awareness of what no concept can conceptualize, i.e. what we have been calling the remainder.

The Self's psychological urge to fully conceptualize its ethical relationship with the Other, without remainder, is frequently based on what Adorno calls the inherently anti-intellectual "wish to be right" (2005: 70). But the wish to be right, in turn, is based not only on a Nietzschean will-to-power, but also on the Self's socially insecure yearning for moral absolution on account of what its concepts "tell" it to do *viz-à-viz* the Other. Hegelian freedom fulfills this desire for absolution by including within itself the freedom not to worry and fret about the moral status of what *Sittlichkeit* excludes as not worth conceptualizing in the first place. Whatever else it may include, this sort of freedom would also give people the right to ignore or expunge

38   *From* ethōs *to ethics*

from memory all the little sufferings of the inconsequential men, women, and children who have stumbled and fell to the side of the road during Spirit's long dialectical march to self-perfection.

At his point in the discussion it is worth recalling that Chapter 1 derived the possibility of an ethics writ large – an ethics of the remainder – from Adorno's critique of Hegelian metaphysics. Such an ethics would necessarily include an attitude of openness to the pre- and nonconceptualized remainder produced by every relationship between Self and Other, as well as a concomitant willingness to let compassion vie with reason in determining one's ethical responses. Seen from the point of view of an ethics that cares about the remainder, the prospect of actually operationalizing the Hegelian quest for a unanimous interpretation of the ethical relationship between Self and Other would be horrifying. At least it would horrify anyone who is not eager to become the equivalent of a well-adjusted, ever-satisfied, and ever-compliant fictional Stepford Wife (Levin, 1972).

What is more, please remember that what is said to be true absolutely cannot in principle be refuted by counterevidence. That is why Wittgenstein, for one, classified metaphysical statements such as Parmenides's, Spinoza's, and Hegel's as neither true nor false, but rather nonsensical (*Unsinn*, or "nonsense") (Wittgenstein, 1968: 28e-29e). Like a hedgehog defensively curling itself into a ball, its spines turned outward, the aggressive absolutism of these expressions seeks to protect them from any possible contradiction, especially any that might come from outside the metaphysical system that generated them. But when they are considered as ordinary propositions, *à la* Wittgenstein, the statements themselves cannot be true precisely because there is no possible circumstance under which they could be false.

Now is not the time to plunge into the dense thicket of Wittgenstein's critique of the nonsensical nature of metaphysical propositions that purport to assert absolute truths. Instead, we would do better to approach the *Is/Ought* distinction from a slightly different angle. In a conversation recorded by the American philosopher O. K. Bouwsma, Wittgenstein once described a striking thought experiment to illustrate the extreme difficulty involved in translating the ordinary grammatical distinction between *Is* and *Ought* from one sociolinguistic context to another, radically different one. The aforementioned movie *The Gods Must Be Crazy* shows and then exploits the phenomenon of cultural differences in the *Is/Ought* relationship for comedic effect. But Wittgenstein's thought experiment goes further: it exhibits the same sort of phenomenon depicted in the movie in order to show the impossibility of even expressing, in universal terms, what those differences are really "about."

Wittgenstein's immediate purpose was to show how little light, if any, is thrown on the nature of the fact/value distinction by philosophical attempts to define value-laden terms like *good*, *right*, and *ethical*. In response to what

From ethōs *to ethics*   39

he took (a bit unfairly) to be British philosopher A. C. Ewing's definition of the word "good" in its moral sense – "Good is what it is right to admire" (1948: 112–17) – Wittgenstein said:

> Imagine a tribe who when they viewed things that were horrible, loathsome to us, clapped their hands, their faces bright, and now they always uttered the word "doog." And now you are to translate the word "doog." How will you translate it? Will you hesitate about this? Wittgenstein was trying to bring out the unsatisfactory character of "I approve." The tribe apparently approves. Will "good" do? I suppose that this involves that the use of the word "good" is affected in some such way as this: That in reference to "good" the use of the word "good" comes to serve also in naming the things that are good. One might be horrified not simply at people's regarding such things as good but also at their calling them good. Simply perhaps this. If we were to translate "doog" into "good," we should be suggesting not simply that they approve of certain things but also that these things are justified by our law, etc. . . . The use of the word "good" is too complicated. Definition is out of the question.
>
> (Bouwsma, 1986: 42)

Wittgenstein liked to use clever thought experiments like this to confound and decenter old prejudices. This particular example imagines that you have been charged with the apparently uncontroversial task of merely *translating* the tribe members' exclamation "Doog!" into English. What difficulties will you experience? On the one hand, if you say " 'Doog!' means 'They approve of this behavior,'" your translation is insufficient because it inadequately conveys the term's clearly intended axiological connotation. The people in question are not in fact giving a sociolinguistic account of what kinds of things they customarily approve of. Rather, they are saying that the behavior in question *really is* . . . what? Answer: *it really is doog*. Put simply, "They approve etc." is not what these people meant when they said "Doog!"

But on the other hand, if you translate "Doog!" as "This behavior *is* morally good," without more, then you are caught on the horns of a dilemma. *First horn*: such a translation leaves the unintended impression that you (the translator) have authoritatively determined that the horrifying behavior in question "really is" morally good (i.e. *Is* = *Ought*), which of course you have not done. *Second horn*: but if you try to say more than this (e.g. by issuing a mild disclaimer), you risk leaving the impression that the textual equation "Doog! = Good!" means that you (the translator) have determined that at least these people's sense of morality is relative to time and place ($Ought_1 \neq Ought_2$). But that adds a meaning to the text that the people themselves did not intend to convey, and thus mistranslates it in a different way.

40 *From* ethōs *to ethics*

It would appear that finding a completely accurate translation of a moral expression like "Doog!" in terms that could be understood, without remainder, by all concerned is like finding a chimera. But that may be because we are looking in the wrong direction. Perhaps the difference between the original ("Doog!") and its most accurate English translation (say, "It is good!") does not belong to the realm of truth or falsity at all. Instead, it may reflect what Walter Benjamin called, in *The Task of the Translator*, two different "modes of intention" (*die Art des Meinens*) about the object or state of affairs that is said to be both *doog* (by the people of the tribe) and *good* (by the translator) (1968: 74). In that case these two modes of intention would resemble two different reports about the same sculpture: one written by a sighted person who could only look at it, the other written by a blind person who could only touch it.

In the "Doog!" example, Wittgenstein employs a plain description of hypothetical facts to cast doubt on the possibility of giving a completely satisfactory *universal* (i.e. metaphysical) definition of the word "good." And yet, rigorous definitions are supposed to be the linguistic manna that practical reason feeds upon. But note: it is not as if Wittgenstein's thought experiment somehow "proves" that moral relativism is true. After all, the assertion "All morality is relative to time and place – there is no universal morality" is itself an absolute metaphysical statement that no amount of counterevidence could disprove. The lesson to be learned from Wittgenstein's thought experiment is far more subtle than that.

The real lesson is that claims of truth and falsity in the sphere of ethics cannot even be fully *understood* in the first place without placing them within the particular sociolinguistic context – i.e. the language-game – in which they occur (see Wittgenstein, 1953: 36e). Indeed, without becoming a Self that somehow has come to be embedded in the very same context. And the phenomenological fact that we just *do* immediately and automatically receive these sorts of claims without thinking about the problematic origins of their routinized applications (and nonapplications) in the society in which we live is not because our faculty of reason is capable of flawlessly bridging the gap between a norm (*Ought*) and its application (*Is*). Rather, the way we actually receive the mode of intention encoded in normative language is both a gift (something good) *and* a curse (something bad) that is bestowed on us by history.

In ethics, those who hesitate are not always lost.

Three cases: compassionless reason, reasonable compassion, and reason versus compassion

The mutilated and/or neglected human remainders left behind by the maneuvers of all rational operations are like the odd bits left over after a

From ethōs *to ethics* 41

baker finishes pressing an enormous sheet of dough into a finite number of regular shapes destined for the oven. Their existence in reality endures, and must be endured by someone, even after the brush of reason sweeps them into the dustbin of history as waste material. Acknowledging the troubling reality of these remainders is an essential precondition for what we have been calling an ethics writ large.

We will therefore end this chapter, and in doing so foreshadow the next, by briefly outlining three ideal-typical ethical situations that will help to clarify what the book means when it talks about the difference between "ethics writ small" and "ethics writ large." We will call the archetypal actors in these situations: (1) the self-regarding rational ethicist; (2) the compassionate rational ethicist; and (3) most important of all, the Self in whom reason is at war with compassion.

The self-regarding rational ethicist

This is someone who happens to feel no compassion for another and is trying to decide, in the moment, whether to do something lawful that he believes will harm the Other – surely a common enough occurrence. If we accept Levinas's idea that the ethical relationship as such always begins when the Self encounters the "face" of the Other in the ethical present (e.g. 1999: 34), then the self-regarding rational ethicist in fact experiences the Other's face as a nasty problem – an impediment to his desires – to be solved by reason alone. Since the anticipated action is not illegal, reason's earlier-noted obsession with controlling lawless liberty makes only one ethical demand of the actor. It demands that he correctly measure his contemplated action against this or that rationally appropriate criterion of ethical rightness. The suspicion never arises in him that his own categorical intuition might be nothing more than the "hypostatized aporia" (Adorno & Benjamin, 1999: 136) of idealism, of someone else's moribund abstractions (e.g. Kant's or Hegel's). In the land of compassionless reason, ethical rightness and wrongness is always a function of a calculation forcing a binary judgment: "Is, or is not, action X consistent with ethical duty (or good character trait) Y?" If the answer is no, then the self-regarding rational ethicist must forbear from doing X. If the answer is yes, then he considers himself free to let the Other be damned and to go full speed ahead with his plans. For reason can feel no need to master "unreasonable" feelings of compassion where there are none.

Thus *endeth* the lesson of ethics according to compassionless reason alone, an ethics writ small, which has no room in itself for rationally unassimilated remainders, whether noticed or unnoticed.

42　*From* ethōs *to ethics*

The compassionate rational ethicist

This is someone in whom reason approves certain legally permissible, other-regarding behavior that compassion is already urging the actor to perform – this is also a common enough occurrence. Now all seems copacetic in the land of ethics, for the horse of reason and the horse of compassion are both pulling in the same direction and have momentum on their side. It only seems that all is well, however, because critical reason knows that practical reason is quite clever. It was Hegel, for example, who first noticed that the empty universality of Kant's Categorical Imperative makes it indeterminate in a real world that is ceaselessly becoming nonidentical with itself as it plunges into the future. "It is only a blunder, an incompetence of reason," he said, if one finds oneself unable to use such a command to justify "any determination and therefore any action at all." If this is so, then "the principle of morality is also the principle of immorality," as the Hegel scholar Jean Hyppolite put it (1996: 57). When compassion and practical reason are aligned, it becomes very hard for critical reason to shake the suspicion that successfully rationalizing a kindness you already want to perform is little more than special pleading by a Self who is too stupid to realize it.

Thus *endeth* the lesson of a different sort of rational ethics writ small: one that is supported, comforted, and whose voice is steered strategically by what compassion already wants to do.

The self in whom reason is at war with compassion

Phenomenally speaking, this Self is conflicted, insecure, and unsure of itself. If reason's message as it is concretely received on a given occasion *tells* the ethical actor to do X at the same time that compassion *urges* him not to do X (or vice versa) – another common enough occurrence – then clearly all is not well in the land of ethics. All is not well because critical reason knows that to bend the knee to practical reason's historically received diktats about how to treat others is to make a moral choice in the ethical present, and yet to follow the contrary urgings of compassionate concern for the Other is also to make a moral choice in the very same ethical present. For it is self-evident that *neither* choice is compelled in advance of the very moment of acting – not by reason, not by compassion, and not by any other imaginary "force" which reason might hypostasize in order to give itself a good conscience. In this situation, the existential burden of making *either* choice is heavy indeed. Hence the Self in this situation suspects that the only fair wage that it can rightly expect to receive for having made the choice will be guilt itself.

Thus *beginneth* the lesson of ethics writ large, whose living trace is only visible in the Self's feeling, always after the fact, that its response to the Other's predicament is an ethical failure as measured by reason, by compassion, or by . . . just about anything and everything else.

Notes

1 From the Greek noun *kharaktēr* (a tool for marking or stamping things (e.g. coins) with words or images).
2 Also known as the Liar's Paradox, this is a logical puzzle that in its most cogent form is produced by the attempt to determine whether the statement "This statement is false" is itself true or false.
3 From the Greek phrase *ta meta ta phusika* ("the things after physics").
4 From the Greek verb *dialegesthai* ("to converse with").

3   The burden of caring

> All interest of my reason (the speculative as well as the practical) is united in the following three questions: **1. What can I know? 2. What should I do? 3. What may I hope?**
>
> Immanuel Kant (1998: 677)

> The limit of language is shown by its being impossible to describe the fact which corresponds to (is the translation of) a sentence, without simply repeating the sentence. (This has to do with the Kantian solution to the problem of philosophy.)
>
> Ludwig Wittgenstein (1977: 10e)

The leading question

Only during the concrete experience of feeling torn between reason and compassion on this or that particular occasion does the ethical relationship as such begin to reveal its true colors. Only then, in the Self's awareness of the potential unethicality of reason *and* the potential unreasonableness of compassion, does what is really at stake in that relationship begin to show itself. On this view, Mark Twain's fictional character Huck Finn (1884) – whose heart told him to help his friend Jim escape from slavery, but whose head told him that he would be damned to hell for doing so – came much closer to grasping the true nature of the ethical relationship than any doctrine or code of ethics, however enlightened, ever has.

We know how Huck resolved his ethical conflict – he helped Jim escape. And we feel *now* that what he did was morally right – that his Kantian "faculty of reason" was pre-shaped by an immoral official *Ought* (respect Miss Watson's "property" rights in Jim) that made him feel guilty unless his conscience could reflexively accept the *Is* of a world in which white people could legitimately make black people their property. We live in a different

The burden of caring 45

world, one in which different sociolegal *Oughts* keep on producing different *Is*'s, and vice versa. They are different *Oughts* and *Is*'s, to be sure, but not categorically different in the ways they construct what human beings take for granted as "normal." If, in *our* world, reason finds itself at war with compassion in a particular ethically charged situation, and if the inner conflict has not yet been resolved, then a knotty ethical problem confronts any ethically conscientious Self who must undergo the ordeal of it.

Let's say you are a U.S. border agent charged with the task of arresting undocumented migrants and refugees. Should you follow policy directives and separate this particular desperate migrant mother from her crying 5-year-old child, or should you pretend you didn't see them and let them both get away? Your head says, "Do your duty: arrest the mother and put the child in a holding facility"; your heart urges you not to brutalize them in the service of a compassionless official policy (see US Department of Justice Policy, 2018). The inquiry that might resolve the problem is less about what you should do than it is about which inner voice (or urge) you should let your body obey. Such an inquiry is precisely what this chapter's leading question initiates. The question is: *which should come first in ethics: reason or compassion?*

Grammatically speaking, "reason or compassion" is like "Coke or Pepsi": the phrase on its face posits two mutually exclusive alternatives. Our leading question thus seems to offer (or force) a choice between two possible foundations – the head or the heart – for living together ethically with others. The choice is framed as binary for a reason. Most notable philosophers, past and present, have expressed a strong preference for the head over the heart in matters of ethics (e.g. Plato and Kant), while a vocal minority of other notable philosophers have gone the other way (e.g. Schopenhauer and Levinas). Before we can try to do justice, so to speak, to Chapter 4's ethical critique of law and justice we must first put the antithesis between the head and the heart to the test of critical reason. Hence, this chapter will continue to build on the ethical critique of the absolute metaphysical distinction, first mentioned in Chapter 1, between rational telling and compassionate urging.

For those inclined to reflexively accept the superiority of reason over compassion, thought over feeling, abstraction over contextualization, being principled over being flexible, and so forth, the answer to our leading question is obvious. If correct moral reasoning tells you to do something that your sense of compassion urges you not to do, then you should always listen to the former and ignore the latter. Contrariwise, the conflict between reason and compassion is resolved the other way around by the liberal Catholic doctrine of *situational ethics*. Although it has taken many forms, situational ethics generally encourages believers to let *agapē* (God's gift of "love for humankind") contradict the stern requirements of ethical legalism *if* the

46 *The burden of caring*

particular situation calls for it (see Borrajo, 1968: 233). If God wants us to temper the rigor of his biblical commands with *agapē*, then who are we to argue? – that seems to be the argument.

Secular faith in the self-evidence of what an ethical norm correctly "tells" the faculty of reason is like religious faith in the "urgings" of *agapē*. Both forms of faith provide the Self with an authoritative ethical excuse – a hall-pass from the school's principal, as it were – which appears somehow to have originated from a source outside of the ethically conscientious Self to authorize and excuse what it is going to do next. Not everyone is a dogmatic rationalist or a nondogmatic Christian, however. For those who do not experience (or even want to experience) the strange alchemy of secular or religious faith in the law-like authority of the faculty of reason or of Christian *agapē*, the conflict between reason and compassion is not so easily resolved. If the road to ethical heaven often seems to belongs to those who obey the telling/urging of a socially or theistically sanctioned *Ought*, these ethically conscientious nonbelievers know that the very same road has frequently led to ethical hell.

Towards a phenomenological interpretation of reason and compassion in ethics

Instead of immediately seeking an answer to our leading question, let's hesitate and go back a step to investigate where the impulse to be other-regarding – the ethical impulse as such – might come from. Whence something emerges into present existence is its origin in the ancient Greek sense of *archē*: the ultimate source – or as Kant would say, the condition of the possibility – of that thing's being what it is. Thus construed, an origin is different from what it originates, but the originated nonetheless would not exist without its origin. In the *Theogony*, for instance, the Greek poet Hesiod claimed that *Chaos* – an unfathomable primordial void – was the *archē* from whence the gods, as well as everything else in the sensible universe, first emerged (1996: 24). A more prosaic factual (i.e. non-metaphysical) example of origin and originated is a river and a waterfall: they are not the same, to be sure, but unless the river flows, there is no waterfall. *That* a waterfall is at all – its sheer existence – is given to it by its origin: a flowing river.

The logical relationship between ethics and the origin of ethics is the same. Although there are plenty of different opinions and theories about how to be an ethical person, they all have the same *archē*, which can be summed up this way: *The origin of ethics is an unwilled and unavoidable burden of caring somehow about the Other that is always borne, and can only be borne, by an individual Self during that ever-replenished here-and-now that we call the present moment.* Although this statement will require

The burden of caring   47

further explanation, its way of framing our inquiry into ethics has the immediate advantage of privileging the "who," "when," and "how" of the ethical relationship over its "what." Or, if you will, attributing ethics to the Self's burden of caring about the Other privileges the lived experience of ethicality (its *thatness*) over a dry doctrinal analysis of the *whatness*, or "essence," of ethics.

The concept of the *burden of caring* is offered as a phenomenological finding,[1] not as a normative prescription or metaphysical assertion. To put this point less formally, the words "burden of caring" merely express a simple observation about human consciousness that can easily be made and verified by engaging in the kind of serious introspection that does not consciously prejudge what it will find. The observation that gives rise to the concept of the burden of caring is just this: look inward and you will find that what happens to other human beings who come within the range of your awareness tends to *matter* to you somehow, at least to some degree or other. From that observation it follows that caring about the Other is not always, or even often, a burden in the Sartrean sense of "Hell is other people" (Sartre, 1989: 45). Rather, it is best characterized as a burden (from the Old English *byrthen*, "to carry") in the value-neutral sense of something that we must sustain, regardless of our preferences, because on any given occasion we probably already are experiencing being-with-others in some way or other, if only in our imagination.

Sometimes the Other's mattering to us shows itself as a selfish desire to use the Other as a means to our own ends, regardless of the consequences to them. Other times the burden of caring shows itself as "an innate repugnance at seeing a fellow-creature suffer," as Rousseau puts it (1993a: 73). Still other times it touches upon the spheres of politics and law, as when the Self desires justice *for* someone or *against* someone else. One might even say that it includes, without being limited to, the struggle for recognition that Hegel described in his chapter on the dialectic of Master and Slave (1977: 111–19). Indeed, there are probably as many different ways of caring about the Other as there are grains of sand on a beach.

Viewed from a Heideggerian perspective, the Self's pre-rational, precompassionate phenomenal burden of caring somehow about the Other within its ken is itself based on a still deeper ontological[2] ground of the Self's existence as a human being. Heidegger famously appropriated German idealism's term for a determinate being of any kind – *Dasein* (literally, "being there") – and made it signify exclusively the being of the human being. Ever fond of neologisms, he also insisted on distinguishing between an "existentiale" determination – a statement identifying an ever-enduring (i.e. absolute) element of the being of Dasein – and a merely "existentiell" (ontic, or factual) statement about the range of possibilities open to Dasein,

48   *The burden of caring*

its understanding of those possibilities, and the choices that it makes (or evades) amongst them (1962: 32–35).

Placing the burden of caring about the Other in a Heideggerian framework would immediately sidetrack our investigations into an ontological discussion of Dasein's "egoicity" (*Egoität*). For Heidegger, egoicity constitutes the pre-ethical ground of what he called being-with-others (*das Mitsein*). The latter was his name for the inescapable sociality that constitutes the "world" of every human being, even on those occasions when he or she happens to be ontically alone (1962: 83). Heidegger's concept of being-with-others, in turn, belongs to his even more general notion of "care" (*die Sorge*), according to which Dasein's always caring about its own possibilities of being is counted as its most fundamental (i.e. absolute) ontological determination (1962: 153–63). He believed that the Self's choice between "egotism and altruism" (including, presumably, what we have called "reason or compassion") in its ethical encounter with the Other is a second order (existentiell) problem that is founded on the first order (existentiale) truth of Dasein's always already first caring about *its own* existential freedom. "Only because Dasein is primarily determined by egoicity," he said, "can it factically exist as a thou for and with another Dasein" (1984: 187).

Heidegger had a lifelong obsession with the question of Being (or "Beyng") as such (*die Seinsfrage*), a question that is associated with the feeling of astonishment that there is anything at all, rather than nothing. But unlike his predecessor Leibniz (1934: 26) or his contemporary Wittgenstein (McGuinness, 1979: 68), both of whom felt the same astonishment on occasion, Heidegger generally avoided asking mundane questions about what existing things (beings) are or might possibly become. We will therefore not follow him into the philosophical domain of thinking Being (*Sein* or *Seyn*), Dasein, and fundamental ontology (*Fundamentalontologie*), no matter how important this line of inquiry might be in other research contexts.

Our phenomenological concept of the Self's somehow caring about the Other has a less lofty aim – one that Heidegger himself would probably have interpreted as being merely existentielle. Even if Heidegger is right that Dasein *is* essentially only its own possibilities of "being futural" (*Zukunftzigsein*) in the now, the distinctly ethical investigation that is framed by this chapter's leading question is designed to uncover *how* these particular possibilities – reason or compassion – actually show themselves in experience. In sum, our leading question does not attempt to shed light on metaphysics or ontology, but rather to enlighten what Heidegger himself called, albeit somewhat condescendingly, the potentially "rich and interesting . . . analysis of possible I-thou relationships" (1984: 187).

That said, we must stress again that the phenomenological category of *caring-about-the-Other* is extremely capacious. All it really means is that

The burden of caring 49

the Other matters to the Self somehow and to some degree, however large or small. Caring is therefore not limited to altruistically "taking care of the Other," and still less to *caritas* in the Christian theological sense of the charitable love of humankind.

As the earlier comparison with grains of sand on a beach suggests, caring covers a vast multiplicity of possible modes of the Other's mattering to the Self somehow and to some degree. Liking, loving, hating, listening-to, talking-to, being-bored-by, making-use-of, having-a-regard-for, desiring-something-from, having-compassion-for, feeling-guilty-towards, resenting, feeling-ambivalent-about, staying-away-from-to-avoid-infecting-with-the-coronavirus, and so forth: all these, and more, are forms of caring about the fate of the Other.

The pre-Socratic philosopher Bias of Priene said that you should love your friends as if you would one day hate them, "since the majority of men are bad" (*pleistoi anthropoid kakoi*) (Diogenes Laërtius, 2018: 43). He did not mention loving and hating rocks or rain puddles. Generally speaking, only if another *human being* comes to our attention in some way or other do these and other possible modes of caring about them jut into consciousness. But since we almost always seem to be perceiving and thinking (or obsessing) about other people – who they are, where they come from, what they think, what they have done, what they will do next, and so forth – the Self's burden of caring about the Other is more or less ceaseless, even in its dreams.

The Jewish philosopher-theologian Martin Buber famously determined the "mutual" (*gegensietig*) nature of the Self's relationship with the Other as one of "I-Thou" (*Ich-Du*), as opposed to "I-It" (*Ich-Es*) (2000: 19–44). Indeed, it is telling that Heidegger's unfortunately unattributed reference to "possible I-thou relationships," quoted earlier, came during a 1928 lecture course that he held five years after the publication in Germany of Buber's masterpiece, *Ich and Du* ("I and Thou"). We invoke Buber's distinction here not as an appeal to the mystical or the mysterious, or even to some alternative (non-Heideggerian) fundamental ontology. The point of drawing attention to it now is simply to reinforce the phenomenological observation underlying the book's thesis that the inner origin of ethics is the Self's burden of caring somehow about the Other. For almost never does a sane person care in any of the previously listed ways about a random rock or rain puddle. Rather, these sorts of caring generally happen only in relation to other human beings.

The burden of caring about the Other should not be confused with the psychic pain of compassion.[3] This is how Arthur Schopenhauer – perhaps the best-known philosopher of compassion in the West – describes the latter emotion's immediate effect on the one who experiences it: "When once

50   *The burden of caring*

compassion [*Mitleid*] is stirred within me by another's pain, then his weal and woe go straight to my heart, exactly in the same way, if not always to the same degree, as otherwise I feel only my own" (2005: 85). For Schopenhauer, this account of what happens inside us when we actually *do* feel compassion for another person implies that the commonly supposed metaphysical difference between Self and Other "is no longer an absolute one." Compassion's partial erasure of the otherwise clear boundary between one person and another, he muses, is "astonishing, indeed hardly comprehensible"; and yet, he claims, compassion alone is the phenomenal origin of "the great mystery of Ethics" (2005: 86).

Schopenhauer's thesis that compassion-as-pain is the true origin of ethics is not the same as the aforementioned interpretation of ethics as originating in an unwilled burden of caring about the Other. For the phenomenon of caring somehow and to some degree about the Other is like a river with many branches. Caring, yes: that is the river before it branches. But caring how – in what way? That is the question *par excellence* of an ethics writ large.

If a particular Self never in fact experiences the pain of compassion for a particular Other, does this really imply or prove that their relationship is wholly ethics-free? Like academic tradition and common sense, we must give a negative answer to this question, even if the path we will take to get there is less conventional than theirs. Our phenomenological interpretation of ethics as something that originates from an unchosen, irremissible, personal burden of caring about the Other takes a step back from Schopenhauer's identification of ethics with compassion to the moment before compassion emerges (or fails to emerge), and, for that matter, before reason can assert (or decline) jurisdiction over what we "should" do. For said burden of caring, like all burdens, can be felt strongly, weakly, or hardly at all, without ever once ceasing to be a burden of caring *somehow*. Instead of constituting the origin of ethics, as Schopenhauer (and perhaps Levinas) thought, unwilled compassion for the Other who suffers is but one possible outcome of that origin.

According to the German theologian Dietrich Bonhoeffer, to experience compassion is "to regard people less in the light of what they do or omit to do, and more in the light of what they suffer" (1977: 10). This way of discussing the inner reality of compassion for another is quite useful because it places the phenomenon's unique mode of intentionality front and center. Considered as a phenomenal state, compassion is characterized primarily by the fact that it is directed *at* (is a consciousness *of*) the essential unity of the Other and its vulnerability. It can be *any* given Other, by the way, regardless of their moral worthiness or lack thereof. This sort of intentionality, in turn, leads to a definition of the word *compassion* that will suffice for our purposes. Compassion is the Self's more-or-less strongly met feeling (a "passion") of pity and concern on account of the Other. You do not

The burden of caring 51

generally acquire compassion for another by willing it into being. Either you come to feel it, or you don't. It follows that "choosing" compassion over reason means letting one's feelings of compassion towards the Other in a particular situation take control of one's actions.

Metaphorically speaking, our leading question interprets the burden of caring as a mighty river that splits into two smaller rivers: compassion and reason. For rational ethics, no less than compassion, also originates from caring somehow about the Other. How, then, should we describe the role of reason in ethics?

Philosophers have traditionally defined reason as "a general faculty, common to all or nearly all [humans]," that comes in two varieties: "a *faculty of intuition* by which one 'sees' truths or abstract things ('essences' or universals, etc.), and a *faculty of reasoning*, i.e. passing from premises to a conclusion (*discursive reason*)" (Lacey, 1986: 201). "Reason" in our leading question generally includes both senses of the word, whether considered alone or in combination. For example, reason *qua* the faculty of intuition, if uncertain of its ethical duties, might discover or give itself ethical rules or moral laws – e.g. "Thou shall (or shalt not) do X" – which reason *qua* the faculty of reasoning could then "follow" by finding and giving reasons (grounds) for what it is about to do.

Reason's proper role in ethics would be easy to describe if, with David Hume, we equated it with instrumental reason. Roughly speaking, instrumental reason is the practical application of the faculty of reasoning from a given premise to a conclusion. Its main function is to figure out the relationship between means and ends. Hume, the leading philosopher of the Scottish enlightenment, believed that the prerational passions, including but not limited to compassion, first tell us what we want (the end), and that only then does reason in the form of the faculty of reason*ing* tell us how (*via what means*) to get what we want. "Reason is, and ought only to be, the slave of the passions," he wrote, "and can never pretend to any other office than to serve and obey them" (1985: 296).

Although Hume's views on morality are far more complex than this one statement might suggest (see Cohon, 2018), we must reject his empiricist theory of mind on ethical grounds. Not because it is bad metaphysics, mind you, but because it would lead our investigations all too quickly into a cozy but unenlightening ethical *cul de sac*. For Humean empiricism risks fostering ethical evasion. For example: if, in fact, you happen to experience compassion for a particular Other, then you will figure out a way to treat them one way, which you will then be able to rationalize as "ethical," *à la* Hume's reason-is-a-slave-of-the-passions metaphor; if you don't have compassion for the Other, then you will figure out another, less kindly way to treat them, and you will also be able to rationalize this other way as "ethical."

52   *The burden of caring*

What our leading question is attempting to ask cannot be evaded so easily. In one way or another, the Kantian distinction between the faculty of reasoning and the faculty of intuition is simply too deeply embedded in our ethical thinking to be overcome by the decision to hide behind anyone's metaphysical barricade, be it called empiricist, idealist, or anything else. Even dyed-in-the-wool empiricists crave a nod of moral approval from their conscience and from others. Experience shows that whenever the ethically conscientious Self decides to do something it knows will harm the Other it generally seeks the comfort of a justification that comes from outside of its own emotional state, its own whims. Its conscience yearns for it to be – or at least to be regarded as – morally right, not just effective at implementing its own desires.

"*Gninnigeb eht ta nigeb*" – George Oppen

If, *pace* Hume, the use of reason in ethical decision-making – i.e. rational intuition *cum* practical reasoning – is seen as a phenomenon in its own right that cannot fairly be reduced to the status of a slave to compassion or any other prerational passion, then the question still remains of how best to characterize its manner of appearance in the ethical present. Let's say you are a judge whose heart urges you to go easy on a particular litigant in a case before you, but whose head keeps nagging you to do your duty by following the celebrated advice of Sir Matthew Hale, Lord Chief Justice of England from 1671 to 1676: "Be not biased with compassion to the poor, or favor to the rich, in point of justice" (Haynes, 1944: 7). Since your heart urges you to be compassionate and your head tells you to be objectively rational – to "follow the law" wherever it leads – it would seem that you have a choice to make.

Our leading question has foreshadowed this kind of situation by asking: which *should* come first in ethics, reason or compassion? "Should" implies the ability to choose between reason and compassion; and the ability to choose, in turn, presupposes the freedom to choose. How does one know that one is free to choose in this sense? A brief look at Immanuel Kant's subtle intellectual maneuverings in response to the latter question will help to clarify what, ethically speaking, our leading question is trying to uncover.

On the one hand, Kant's *Third Antinomy* shows that reason cannot "prove" the transcendental reality of freedom without contradicting itself – we are free *and* we are not free – in a world where creatures such as us are also governed by natural necessity (1996: 484–85). On the other hand, Kant also insists that morality means the practical ability to govern one's actions on the basis of law-giving reason alone, and not desire (1996: 166–67). Lest moral freedom be left hanging in the air without any metaphysical

The burden of caring   53

foundation, he famously posits it as a "regulative idea": that is, belief in the idea of freedom (somehow) licenses us to think of ourselves *as if* our will were autonomous and therefore unburdened by natural causation (1996: 179). On this view of freedom, the ability to choose in the moral sphere rests not on logic or evidence, but rather on what Kant himself revealingly called "rational faith" (*Vernunftglaube*) (2014).

Inasmuch as Kant defines morality as a function of law-giving reason alone, it is unsurprising that the kind of rational faith he prefers will necessarily choose reason over compassion in matters of ethics. In any ethically charged situation where law-governed reason urges us to do one thing and the feeling of compassion urges us to do the opposite, Kant seems to have stacked the deck of choice in such a way that we are commanded in advance to discard the card of compassion from the hand that fate has dealt us. Linguistically speaking, however, Kant's concept of "rational faith" in freedom of choice is internally, not externally, related to his stipulated ethical duty to choose reason over compassion whenever the two are in conflict. That is, no amount of evidence from experience could have convinced him to resolve the conflict differently. The only thing in Kant's moral philosophy that prevents us from investigating how ethical choice *as such* shows itself phenomenally in individual experience is an inter-propositional diktat based on Kant's prerational faith in the absolute ethical rightness of choosing reason over compassion in all cases.

Well then, let's just assume for the moment that in matters of ethics the will does have the practical freedom to choose between reason and compassion – either reason over compassion or compassion over reason – and then, without prejudging the outcome the way Kant does, see where this assumption leads us.

Hannah Arendt's idea of freedom provides a useful point of departure for this inquiry into freedom of choice in the ethical sphere. She realized that before primordial freedom can be talked about as something that is enhanced or diminished by political circumstances, it must first be seen and understood in its own right. So, she defined freedom as the power to initiate a "new beginning": a moment in time in which we are (somehow) able to break free of forces from the past and found something new in the living present (1958: 202). Seen from this standpoint, our leading question seems to presuppose the practical possibility of (1) momentarily damming the incessant flow of history's forces during a given face-to-face encounter with another person and then (2) authoritatively deciding to put our head in command of our heart, or our heart in command of our head.

If this is our definition of practical freedom, however, the odd-looking epigram quoted at the head of this section, which seems to be written in *some* kind of language, casts more than a little doubt on the plausibility

54   *The burden of caring*

of our leading question's implicit assumption that choosing a rational new beginning is categorically different from choosing a compassionate one. The sentence "*Gninnigeb eht ta nigeb*" – and it *is* a sentence – wryly mocks the thesis that one can begin to understand, let alone decide upon, anything at all during some autochthonous beginning in which one could choose to remain magically uncontaminated by the push and pull of historical forces. Here the American poet George Oppen, whose *Daybooks* contain numerous references to Heidegger, inscribes *backwards* his own, pseudo-Arendtian epigram about beginning at the beginning (2007: 176).

As it happens, Oppen's epigram subtly illustrates Heidegger's famous theory of *Befindlichkeit*: the insight that at any given moment each of us finds ourselves always already inhabited by a preexisting mood (*Stimmung*) and a pre-theoretical understanding (*Vorgriff*) of the way things are and are supposed to be, *before* ever explicitly setting out to make sense of the world (including especially ourselves). The existential truth of our always already having been thrown into a preexisting world (*Geworfenheit*, or "thrownness," as Heidegger called it), thus suggests that the causes of our comprehending – or failing to comprehend – anything whatsoever are already secretly underway in us before the beginning of any attempt to understand it that we might consciously initiate (1962: 175).

Less obviously, but more importantly for present purposes, Heidegger's thesis implies that the mood of compassion emerges in us as a lived phenomenon in pretty much the same way a given instance of rational understanding emerges: momentarily pushed above the waterline of the ethical present by a submerged substrate of past forces and conditions of which we remain largely unaware. Considered as purely temporal phenomena, spontaneously feeling concern for a baby when it starts to cry, spontaneously understanding what the linguistic signs *Begin at the beginning* signify without having to look up the words in the dictionary, and spontaneously feeling puzzled upon first encountering the linguistic signs *Gninnigeb eht ta nigeb*, all belong to the same order of experience: the seamless feeling of immediacy.

The irreducible immediacy of understanding (or not understanding) in the linguistic realm is the precise analog of an unpremeditated outburst of emotion. The linguistic immediacy of understanding is a phenomenon that we have already referred to as "reception." It is characterized by the effortless absorption of language, like a sponge absorbing water, unpreceded by anything that could fairly be called a rational "act" of understanding it. Experienced from the point of view of the linguistic receiver, or actor, interpretation is a function of perceived unclarity or ambiguity. It is often a conscious choice between possible alternatives: text "X" means Y, not Z. A lack of clarity or ambiguity must first be noticed, however, before it can lead to a mental act of interpretation. Our grammatical conventions give *others*

The burden of caring   55

(observers) who do notice a textual ambiguity the right to say, "That's just his interpretation." But if the actor himself unreflectively received, in univocal terms, what the text "tells" him, then the fact that an observer construes what he said and did with it as "merely an interpretation" does not imply that the actor himself also experienced a discrete mental act of interpretation.

The foregoing claim of irreducible immediacy in the everyday reception of language is not the product of some hoity-toity theory of discourse. We can easily understand both the claim and its ethical significance by paying close attention to what happens – and more importantly, to what does *not* happen – during our most banal experiences with words. Texts that we experience as unclear or ambiguous can always be interpreted, of course, but even then – *especially* then – the mental act of interpreting them will eventually cease, after which I just know how to go on. Or rather, I then just *do* go on in a certain way, having been (somehow) prodded in that direction by words and their associated images. Honest introspection will find no rule-like rational "mortar" joining the brick of a verbal prescription (rule, norm, principle, etc.) to the brick of its real application in the living present. Instead, the most that can be found and truthfully reported is the fact that "*I* [emphasis added] have already to read a certain kind of application into the expression" (McGuinness, 1979: 155, quoting Wittgenstein).

That is what the phenomenon called "rationally understanding language" looks like in reality: adopt whatever model or scheme of interpretation you want, it will in fact eventually terminate at a level that is made up of still more linguistic signs; then, as Wittgenstein says, "there will be no such thing as an interpretation of that" (1978: 34). There will just be an action, or better still, the only thing that will show itself in reality is the unadorned phenomenon of someone just *acting*. "In the beginning was the deed," as we said in Chapter 1, quoting Goethe's Faust. This is not just a glib slogan. It is reason's ethical admission to itself, at long last, that "[r]epresented in the inmost cell of thought is that which is unlike thought" (Adorno, 1973: 408).

What is unlike thought, but still *in* thought, is what makes ethical thought possible. It is not necessarily the lurking influence of unseemly "biases" engendered by compassion, hatred, factionalism, or any other emotion. Inside the inmost cell of thought lie the coiled, preconscious springs of customary ways of receiving language as they wait to be triggered in the ethical present. Are these customary ways of receiving language always (or ever) sufficient to justify and excuse the Self who lets them loose on the Other, for good or ill? "In the beginning was the deed" describes the very moment of ethics itself – a moment in which thought reaches the end of its rope and therefore forfeits all assurance of excuse or justification.

Professional ethics, religious ethics, and philosophical ethics, to the extent they concern themselves with discussions of ought and ought-not, are

56 *The burden of caring*

parachronistic: they belong to a time that is always earlier than the ethical present. Linguistic normativity consists of words that were thought, written, read, and understood in a past that always precedes the messy irruption, right now, of any particular ethically questionable deed. In short, any actual act of measuring or adjudicating with an ethical norm to reach some sort of conclusion or result – where the rubber hits the road, so to speak – always comes to pass in some particular Self's very own ethical present. As Wittgenstein suggests, this difference in the temporality of *artifactual ethical norms* and that of *living ethical deeds* creates an unilluminated logical space that no amount of words can close.

Adorno once said, "When all actions are mathematically calculated, they also take on a stupid quality" (2005: 107). If stupidity means acting automatically – as an effect of a cause – then we are all of us stupid. That is why at the end of the day an ethics writ small makes stupidity even stupider without ever once acknowledging it. The mortar that joins any ethical norm or principle to what we actually *do* with it is never rightness itself, but always only some *Me-Myself* acting (or not acting) in a moment that can be freighted with a moral significance that I may or may not recognize. It is a moral significance that I usually do not recognize, in fact, as I sleepwalk with all the other sleepwalkers through a landscape that our dreams keep prettifying to keep us from gawking in horror at the spectacle of violence, poverty, despair, and suffering all around us.

By means of the many social-historical mechanisms (*Is*'s) that were discussed in Chapter 2, each of us ultimately comes to "read" or "hear" only certain kinds of applications (*Oughts*) into ethical prescriptions, and, for that matter, into any type of artifactual norm that we have come to accept as authoritative. According to an ethics writ large, however, there is no additional rational principle or ground that could ever save us from the gritty existential task of making – or rather enduring – such a reading or hearing. That is why our leading question's premise – the freedom to choose between reason and compassion – is misleading.

The moral thesis that the will is free actually coincides with the amoral thesis that it is unfree, because they both proclaim, falsely, that sensible reality itself is governed *ab initio* by the principle of identity (cf. Adorno, 1973: 264). They both falsely proclaim that there can be no ethically troubling particularities, no remainders, that compassion might detect inarticulately in the ethical present, but that reason cannot squeeze into the unity of a conceptual determination to be explained away. As Adorno remarked, reason's ideal combines an appetite for incorporation with an aversion to what cannot be incorporated (1973: 161). And yet, mystery of ethical mysteries, somehow compassion is able to sense, every now and then, that what persists outside the sphere of reason's recognition is always more than it could ever be inside any concept.

The burden of caring 57

Adorno's pithily summarized his book-length critique of the principle of identity in a way that could not be more useful for our purposes: "What is, is more than it is" (1973: 161). This suggests a thesis that is embarrassing and unflattering to reason's traditional feeling of superiority over emotion. The thesis is that reason and emotion, head and heart, *both* lie at the mercy of historical forces that they cannot, as a matter of principle, master in advance. When seen from this point of view, the rational, compassion-supressing deduction made by preachers in the antebellum South that Scripture proves that God likes slavery (see Rae, 2018), and Huck Finn's compassionate, guilt-inducing effort to help his friend Jim escape from slavery (Twain, 1884), have pretty much the same etiology.

All of which implies, in turn, that the correct answer to the question whether reason or compassion will in fact come first in any given ethically charged situation is just this: if either one *does* emerge first, this will be because it just happened on that particular occasion to win a murky underwater race with all its competitors, including the feeling of indifference, to the surface of our consciousness.

Responsibility versus presponsibility: herein of Levinas

The formal structure of traditional ethical discourse is quite literally reactionary. It holds that the sense of compassion, when properly controlled by reason, lies (and should lie) dormant in the individual subject, who is otherwise morally free to pursue their own interests and desires in good conscience unless and until the ethical impulse to care about the fate of the Other is animated by the right circumstances. The ethical impulse, when dressed in its conventional garb, is responsible in the precise etymological sense of the Latin infinitive *respondēre*: it stands ready to "answer back" to the predicament of another person, but only *after* the ethical actor has judged the Other's situation worthy of self-restraint or positive intervention according to some normative criterion of worthiness. Such a view of ethical responsibility is premised on a legalistic and reciprocal conception of moral duty: I owe you the exact same moral consideration that you owe me, neither more nor less, and vice versa. All excess compassion be damned!

Interestingly enough, the origin of our word "norm" and "normative" is the Latin noun *norma*, which signifies a carpenter's square: a tool for measuring and marking timber for cutting. A means to an end, in other words. The norms of normative ethics – ethics writ small – operate in an analogous way. They are verbal means or tools, made in advance, for planning and selecting the most ethically correct future course of action, or for adjudicating whether a particular past action should be praised as ethical or condemned as unethical. As in the Hegelian theory of *Sittlichkeit*, ever more

58 *The burden of caring*

nuanced refinements in normative phraseology and argumentation come to resemble improvements in the tools of carpentry: they invite us to think of what everyone around us accepts as moral progress as if it were a kind of technological advancement in our collective selves. The hive-mind of moral consensus "will rise above the particular and cleanse it of all that resists the concept" (Adorno, 1973: 173). And whatever irregular remainders are generated by moral progress in normativity will just fall to the floor like wood shavings.

In reaction to this cabinetmaker's view of normative ethics, many of us have come to believe, to quote the French philosopher Jacques Derrida, that "the way we define ethics today is shaking on its lack of foundations" (2016: 24). Those who inwardly cling to the possibility of discovering secure rational foundations for right conduct – including most especially the decision to inflict "just" suffering on others in good conscience – sometimes reproach postmodern discourse about ethics, law, and politics as dangerously immoral and irresponsible. But for those who feel themselves shaking on a lack of foundations in these spheres, it is the very decision to bestow unqualified trust in the traditional categories of responsibility in ethics, law, and politics that comprises the worst act of moral irresponsibility.

Chapter 2's investigation into the codependency of *Is* and *Ought* tried to show that whatever it is that rational ethical norms seem to "tell" us in the ethical present sits squarely atop the cabinet-like catafalque of history. On this view of ethicality, *ethōs* in the ancient Greek sense of social custom and *ethics* in the modern sense of rule-governed individual behavior merge with one another in the same way that lignin and carbohydrate combine to make wood. Like Walter Benjamin's figure of the Angel of History, where others see a mere chain of events, and even progress, the ethically disillusioned postmodern Self "sees one single catastrophe which keeps piling wreckage upon wreckage and hurls it in front of his feet" (1968: 257).

It is no mystery why the Angel of History, who has quietly observed human suffering throughout the ages, first came to Benjamin's attention in 1940, only a few months before he committed suicide at the Franco-Spanish border while trying to escape from the Nazis. Ever since World War II – and less visibly, since the beginning of human history – far too great a proportion of human wreckage piled at the feet of the Angel of History has been hurled there by the instrumentally rational calculations of compassionless armies, politicians, movements, and factions. It seems like only yesterday, for example, that at least some officials in the U.S. Public Health Service sincerely believed that the horrific Tuskegee syphilis experiment (1932–72) – in which African American men infected with syphilis were left untreated to observe the natural progression of the disease while being told they were receiving free health care – was sound public policy (see Jones, 1993).

The burden of caring 59

What to do? Enter Emmanuel Levinas. This philosopher's unceasing emphasis on the affective dimension of the existentially concrete and unrepeatable face-to-face encounter between two human beings (a Self and an Other) has made it possible to think about the ethics of law and politics in terms of what might be called a radically asymmetrical *pre*sponsibility, to coin a useful neologism. The notion of presponsibility stands opposed to the aforementioned traditional Western conception of reactive responsibility. Presponsibility signifies a way of thinking about ethical responsibility that removes it from the Kantian category of a duty dependent upon rational reflection – a process that requires temporal duration – and places it (to quote Derrida) in a category that is "prior to the senses and to their performative orientation" (2016: 90).

The concept of presponsibility advances the claim that each one of us always already bears a burden of guilt and responsibility because of the actual or possible suffering of the Other – *any* given other whom we face – without reference to the acknowledgment or proof of some discrete act of wrongdoing on our part. In short, the word *presponsibility* is but another way of expressing the Self's nascent impulse to ethicality. On any given occasion that impulse belongs to – but may or may not emerge from – what we earlier called the Self's unwilled, unavoidable burden of caring (somehow) about the Other.

Perhaps the apotheosis of presponsibility *becoming* reasonless compassion is a phenomenon that Levinas, following the novelist Vasily Grossman, calls "senseless kindness." Kindness is senseless when compassion's urgings inexplicably overcome reason's demand that kindness be withheld in the service of some other end. What is more, this sort of kindness is by definition ungeneralizable. It shows itself as

> the "small goodness" from one person to his fellowman that is lost and deformed as soon as it seeks organization and universality and system, as soon as it opts for a doctrine, a treatise of politics and theology, a party, a state, and even a church. Yet it remains the sole refuge of the good in being. Unbeaten, it undergoes the violence of evil, which, as small goodness, it can neither vanquish nor drive out. A little kindness going only from man to man, not crossing distances to get to the places where events and forces unfold! A remarkable utopia of the good or the secret of its beyond.
>
> (1998: 230)

A compassionate kindness lacking in the means to explain and justify itself is nonrational, even if it might also be called instrumentally irrational. The philosopher Bettina Burgo, in her article on Emmanuel Levinas for the *Stanford Encyclopedia of Philosophy*, has written that if ethics is defined

60 *The burden of caring*

conventionally as following principles, calculating utility, or cultivating virtue, "then Levinas's philosophy is not an ethics" (2011). It is certainly not any kind of ethics writ small. But we must steadfastly resist any effort to axiomatize ethics in such a way as to banish from philosophy what thinkers like Levinas have to say about it. Perhaps the greatest lesson to be learned from Levinas is the need to resist ethical indifference. What our reason pre-certifies as the "necessary" suffering of others must *never* become an ethically neutral category for us, even as we go about tolerating and inflicting it in our daily lives. Kant's desire to know "What should I do?" (1998: 677), as an end, explains why reason posits ethical criteria for itself, as a means. Adhering rigorously to those criteria in the ethical present, however, does not imply that an ethically correct conscience is, or should be, a good conscience.

Levinas referred to what we have been calling presponsibility in the relationship between Self and Other as "the idea of the infinite" (1996: 19). He said that the immediate consequence of this impulse is a burdensome but morally necessary sense of "guilt without fault" (2001: 52). For Levinas, human existence itself is without any reason or basis that reason, in the mode of the faculty of rational intuition, could discover. It is therefore quite literally unjustifiable. It follows that each one of us stands in need of forgiveness merely on account of the fact that we exist.

> My "being in the world" or my "place in the sun," my home – have they not been the usurpation of places belonging to others already been oppressed by me or starved, expelled to a Third World: rejecting, excluding, exiling, despoiling, killing? "My place in the sun," said Pascal, "the beginning and the archetype of the usurpation of the entire world." Fear for all that my existence – despite its intentional and conscious innocence – can accomplish in the way of violence and murder.
>
> (Levinas, 1999: 23)

Rational ethics strives to be finite (i.e. limited in advance) by what it takes its linguistic norms to "mean" before they are applied. In contrast, the concept of infinite ethical responsibility for the Other, before and beyond any prior judgment or rational calculation, uses the word *infinite* in the etymologically precise sense of *not-finite*. That is, the notion of *pre*sponsibility must be left intentionally amorphous if it is to do us any good as the basis for a thoughtful step back from the ordinary concept of ethical *re*sponsibility. The concept of ethical presponsibility must always steadfastly refuse to submit to any prior analytical definition or limitation of its "content," lest it be confused with ethical *non*-responsibility, or, worse still, ethical *ir*responsibility as determined by the privative application of abstract norms.

For centuries, theologians in all three Abrahamic religions have used apophasis[4] as a rhetorical technique to indicate the perfect goodness of God by

The burden of caring   61

saying clearly what he is *not*. For example, when Maimonides said, "It is a false assumption to hold that He [הוה] has any positive attribute," he did not mean to say that there is no God. He meant to *indicate* the opposite without *saying* it (2011: 62). If theologists can attempt to adumbrate God by saying what he is not, then we ought to be able to elucidate ethics, too, as what remains morally troublesome – what nags our consciences, in fact – about our relations with others even after all our conventional concepts of ethics have been tallied and understood, and even after our own actions have been pronounced ethically correct. There is a big difference, though, between negative theology and what Chapter 1 called "negative ethics" (a synonym for an ethics writ large). The former asks people to put their religious faith in "what-cannot-be-said" – i.e. in the absolute goodness and omnipotence of God – whereas the latter asks only that secular faith in the unquestioned wisdom of rational ethics be suspended on account of what it *leaves out* and what it does *not* accomplish.

It follows that ethical presponsibility should not be thought of as an infinite number of ethical acts, and still less as an inchoate moral duty to perform such acts. It is better characterized as the indeterminate possibility of *noticing* the many sorts of human suffering that the single-minded pursuit of rational ethics causes us to overlook. "What the eye doesn't see, the heart doesn't grieve over," remarked Wittgenstein, channeling the sixteenth-century Catholic saint Teresa of Avila (1983: 205). If only the eye that sees can grieve because of what it sees, then this book's gesture of drawing attention to infinite ethical presponsibility represents a moral wager on the proposition that the more suffering we are able to see, the wider the circle of our actual ethical concern will become. And possibly, just possibly, our presponsibility will ripen into a different kind of ethical responsibility. Rather than solving prepackaged ethical problems, the notion of presponsibility, derived from Levinas, seeks to uncover them as what they are: hard ethical dilemmas.

The politics of ethics writ large

Now it is undeniable, and certainly understandable, that learning how to work within and around the norms of professional responsibility, as well as knowing how to navigate in the choppy waters of conventional ethical arguments, are matters of great practical importance for lawyers, judges, politicians, and citizens, all of whom are involved, in one way or another, in the creation, maintenance, and enforcement of laws and the legal system. After all, we know that many a once-respected esquire has been shunned, fined, suspended, disbarred, and/or removed from office for violating official ethical norms. Nevertheless, and to repeat one last time: the present volume has nothing to do with improving professional and/or philosophical ethics in the ordinary senses of these terms.

62 *The burden of caring*

And why not? Why not always choose to help people find the generally correct ethical path to follow in their future dealings with others? In short, why not try to peddle yet another ethics writ small?

It has been a central premise of this book that you cannot successfully place the immoral parts or structurally unjust effects of a legal system into an airtight ethical quarantine if your purpose is to let yourself perform all of your other legally required or permissible tasks in good conscience. Once you have seen or felt that a given system of control creates or tolerates cruel, needless suffering, you cannot just choose to unsee and unfeel it. A good conscience is by definition a self-satisfied conscience. But a self-satisfied conscience is also ethically stupid, and to believe otherwise is a form of ethical self-delusion.

A prime example is the formal rules of professional responsibility for lawyers. If trying to do justice in good faith counts as "being ethical" so long as legal actors correctly follow the professional codes of good behavior they find online or printed in bar association pamphlets, then ethical discourse itself becomes, in effect, a tawdry exercise in moral apologetics for whatever revolting background conditions the ethical codes themselves take for granted. That explains why the Axiom of Legal Progress identified in Chapter 1 is so dangerous. Once again, the axiom reads, in all of its faux glory: **The ethically correct enforcement of just law is always good and desirable.** But is it *always* good and desirable to reduce ethics to law's handmaiden if you and everyone else think it is just? Or is it not *sometimes* an invitation to collaborate in what Robert Cover called "a system of oppression" (1984: 6)? An ethics writ small has a hard time even asking these questions in the first place, let alone answering them – a point that will be revisited and reinforced in Chapter 5's discussion of the classic juridical problem of "fidelity to law."

Intellectual integrity, epistemological modesty, and above all, a decent regard for the competing ethical claims of reason and compassion do not allow us to take the law's background conditions for granted here. Those conditions are not neutral historical forces or social engines that push, willy-nilly, countless real situations into inherently context-transcending (universal) ethical categories established by reason. Law's background conditions first mutilate those situations by leaving behind remainders in reality that only compassion – not the prideful faculty of reason – is capable of acknowledging without losing face.

The idea that a belief can continue to produce powerful effects even after people cease believing in it is most closely associated with the work of Max Weber. He noted that the feeling of duty in one's calling continues to remain the basis of capitalism's social ethic even though a universal, all-abiding faith in the Calvinist foundation of worldly asceticism that gave rise to it has largely

The burden of caring 63

disappeared. "The idea of duty in one's calling prowls about in our lives like the ghost of dead religious beliefs," Weber remarked, so much so that "the [modern] individual generally abandons the attempt to justify it at all" (1976: 182).

If, today, the moral duty to work in one's calling is the ghost of dead religious beliefs, then the tendency to reduce all of ethics to rational ethics can be seen as the ghost of a dying secular belief in reason's infallibility. For something enormous has happened to the world to explain why the notion of an ethics writ large is even imaginable in the first place. After Auschwitz, widespread faith in reason *qua* the rational intuition of universal essences is dead or dying. But the use of reason *qua* the faculty of reason*ing* goes on and on, for without it nothing whatever could ever be made intelligible. Even the sort of radical deconstruction that allows language to show itself to the reader as always already multivocal with respect to its own possibilities needs to make use of the discursive faculty of reasoning from premise to conclusion in order to demonstrate the many paths that might have been taken from a given textual premise.

But why would anyone even want to demonstrate the paths that might have been taken, or that still might be taken, from where we stand now, in the ethical present? Generally speaking, the motivation to criticize the established, taken-for-granted order of things comes from two sources: the desire to *change* the way things are, and the desire to *understand* the way they are. Call the first the "revolutionary impulse," and the second the "truth impulse."

Marx's eleventh thesis on Feuerbach expresses the revolutionary impulse quite succinctly: "The philosophers have only interpreted the world differently; the point is to change it" (1959: 245). Embedded in this famous thesis is an unconscious subversion of the ground on which the truth impulse stands. Unconscious because Marx, like most other thinkers of his era, believed that he knew the world for what it really was behind the fog of nineteenth-century superstition and ideology. Today his words can be read to imply that believing the world is knowable as it "really is," by him or anyone else, is not just ineffectual in itself. Such a belief also fails to comprehend that *any* mere description of the way things are is already just another "interpretation" standing next to all the other interpretations made throughout human history. Interpretations alone can do nothing on their own, and so Marx clearly means to say that although they may be a means to the end of doing, they should never be thought of as ends in their own right. It is changing the world that is the proper end of the revolutionary impulse, and not just blabbing about it.

But what if the revolutionary impulse cannot be activated without the truth impulse having first prepared the way? What if believing that one has understood the world correctly – including all of its unjust oppressions, together with their causes and conditions – is a necessary condition for the

64 *The burden of caring*

revolutionary impulse to become kindled in the first place? In that case a kind of paradox would emerge. The impulse to change the world for the better, grounded in the undeniable truth of the need for change, would have to cut itself adrift from merely *bearing witness* to unjust human suffering in order to *design and enact* revolutionary change aimed at alleviating that suffering. But *tempus fugit*, and in cutting itself loose, the Self would lose the ability, or at least the will, to bear witness to all the unacknowledged suffering that is happening around it while it is busily changing the world through the use of instrumental reason. It would become invested in not seeing facts that would undermine its own existence as a revolutionary impulse (see Mannheim, 1985: 40).

The truth impulse says, "Slow down – not so fast – maybe you're doing more harm than good," whereas the revolutionary impulse says, "Forward now to change the bad things in the world!" The revolutionary impulse, if it needs the truth impulse as its necessary ground, also does not need – indeed, may be killed by – subsequent irruptions of the truth impulse in the form, say, of the desire to see "the tears that a civil servant cannot see" (Levinas, 1996: 23). For post-revolutionary justice needs civil servants too.

Kant famously said, "Thoughts without intuitions are empty, intuitions without concepts are blind" (1998: 193–94). Something similar can be said about the ethics in relation to law and justice. Criticism of the established order that is not informed by the desire to bear witness to human suffering is blind, but criticism that answers only to the impulse to discover and recognize such suffering is ineffectual. Lying somewhere in between these two states is always the individual Self, acting as a *Me-Myself* in the only time it will ever have to do, or forbear from doing, anything whatsoever. That time is the ethical present, the only possible venue for an ethics writ large, which might also be called an anti-politics, or better still, a politics writ small.

Notes

1 Roughly speaking (*very* roughly speaking), phenomenology is the philosophical discipline of attempting to accurately describe the Self's inner experience ("phenomenon") of being conscious of (and thus "intending") any object, X, that can be subjectively experienced as such, *as* an X.

2 In keeping with a philosophical usage made famous by Heidegger, an "ontological" (*ontologisch*) interpretation of something is a description of its manner of being – "being" in the sense of the present participle of the verb *to be*, rather than in the sense of a gerund denoting a particular kind of entity (*a* human being, for example). A factual statement about *what* a particular being is, or *that* it exists, is called *ontic* or *ontical* (*ontisch*). An *ontological* account, in contrast, aims to describe *how* a being in the ontic sense both comes to be and perdures, i.e. exists through time.

3 From the Latin compound verb *compati*, meaning to suffer (*pati*) with (*com*).

4 From the Greek verb *apophemi*, "to say no."

4 Ethical doubts about justice

[B]eing asked what city was best modelled, "That," said Solon, "where those that are not injured try and punish the unjust as much as those that are."

Plutarch (1950: 95)

Quis custodiet ipsos custodes? ("Who will guard the guardian?")

Juvenal (2004: 266)

The hope for justice

The Nobel Laureate Nigerian playwright Wole Soyinka was asked in a recent interview whether any particular African nation gave him hope for justice, democracy, and economic fairness in that continent. He replied:

I no longer use the word "hope." I just look at the records of the past, the advances made since then, and the evidence of sincerity in the policies that are set. Hope, despair, and so on – I've moved completely beyond that.

(Soyinka & Gates, 2019: 34)

Not many human beings are capable of stoically transcending the conceptual dualism hopeful/hopeless and its close relative, optimism/pessimism, as completely as Soyinka appears to have done. Most prefer – or as Nietzsche thought, are impelled (1968: 451) – to hope. And it is quite remarkable – touching, even – how many of these hopers extend their concerns far beyond the sphere of their own personal and familial interests to include everyone else, including even the welfare of strangers suffering injustice in strange lands. Countless hopers have imagined that their strong desire for the establishment of justice on earth – or at least a better kind of justice than exists now – can and will someday be fulfilled.

66   *Ethical doubts about justice*

Enter the law, for law seen as a means to the ends of justice typically plays a very substantial role in their imaginings. More precisely, these hopers are convinced that the seemingly endless story of the law's uneasy relationship with justice will nevertheless have a happy ending. They believe this despite the gruesome counterevidence provided by countless historical horrors in which the ordinary or malevolent use of laws and the legal system helped midwife the outcomes: the Inquisition, the European conquest and colonization of the Americas, the Middle Passage, American slavery followed by the Jim Crow era, the Holocaust, the Soviet Gulag, the Rwandan genocide, to name but a few. They believe this no matter how dark and depressing things seem to be at the moment: the alarming political successes of climate change denialism; ceaseless wars in the Middle East; ever-increasing impunity for human rights violations; the Brexit imbroglio; the heightened nationalism, racism, and misogyny of MAGA-themed Trumpism; Gilded-Age levels of income inequality; the alarming resurgence of authoritarian, neo-fascist political parties around the world; etc.

The hope for justice in the face of so much pain and disappointment explains why most people would probably agree that the Axiom of Legal Progress, first mentioned in Chapter 1, is and should be noncontroversial: **The ethically correct enforcement of just law is always good and desirable.** As was noted then, however, perhaps the axiom's greatest ethical danger comes from the very fact that it, or any plausible variation of it, seems so self-evidently true to so many people. For truths congealed into unquestionability by consensus are like a hail of bullets let loose by a company of soldiers standing in a skirmish line: sometimes they hit the target, sometimes they don't.

A picture is worth a thousand words, they say, so let's take a look at one. Seen from the point of view of those who accept the obvious truth and wisdom of the Axiom of Legal Progress, the relationships between *law*, *justice*, and *ethics* resemble the relationships between the parts of a skinny isosceles triangle.

According to the Hegelian concept of *Sittlichkeit*, discussed in Chapter 3, the eventual convergence of law, justice, and ethics that is depicted at the top of Figure 4.1 below is inevitable – the outcome of an inalterable law of history. The apex (**Justice**) represents what the nineteenth-century mathematician-philosopher Antoine-Augustin Cournot called the "end of history" (*fin de l'histoire*) (Featherstone, 1993: 184). It was Hegel's and Cournot's interpretation of human history as an ultimately benign teleological process that Francis Fukuyama appropriated in his popular 1992 book *The End of History and the Last Man*, which argues (prematurely in hindsight) that the dissolution of the Soviet Union presaged the absolute triumph of Western liberal democracy as the world's only remaining form of human government (Fukuyama, 2006).

Ethical doubts about justice 67

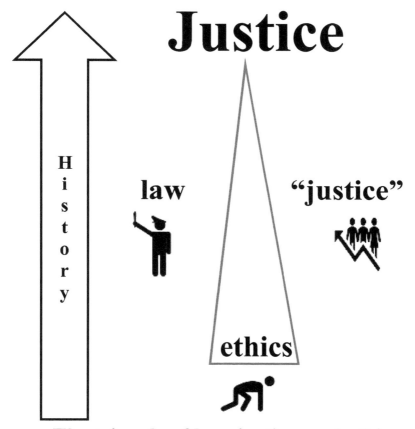

Figure 4.1 The triangle of law, justice, and ethics

As depicted here, however, Figure 4.1 makes no predictions about the future. It merely shows what those who believe in the Axiom of Legal Progress *hope* will occur. The passage of time (as History) flows vertically from the base to the apex of this triangle. The base represents (1) normative ethics, or ethics writ small. The two sides represent (2) law as it is actually being enforced through history and (3) some hoped-for ideal or concept of "justice." The sides are depicted as nonconcurrent but congruent because what is legal can be unjust and what is just can be illegal, and therefore the two concepts must be kept analytically distinct from one another even as the distance between them will grow ever narrower, so it is hoped, as a result

68 *Ethical doubts about justice*

of individuals (who else?) repeatedly acting to apply the Axiom of Legal Progress to enough real situations. The legal philosopher Lon Fuller gave voice to the sort of upbeat, secular optimism that seems to imbue this hope with a certain degree of plausibility: "If we do things the right way," he said, "we'll do the right things" (Fuller, 1948: 204).

Now let us look at justice from an instrumental point of view. If ongoing injustice seems to present itself all at once, so to speak, in the form of a disreputable end-state that has or may come to pass, in one way or another, then justice is never simply a good state of affairs that happens to exist. According to the Axiom of Legal Progress, justice needs to exhibit a blameless pedigree. It must not only *be* a good state of affairs, but also be one that has *come about* in the right way, through just means. What might otherwise be seen as a just punishment, for example, becomes unjust if it is inflicted by the wrong sort of person (Hampton, 1984). Justice, like the Roman god Janus, has two faces: one substantive (the end), the other procedural (the means). And like Janus, the god of beginnings and endings, there is a sense in which justice at once looks forward in time to its future arrival (as *being* a just end), and yet also backward in time at the means of its accomplishment (as *having become* just through just means). Unlike the act of recognizing injustice, the act of hoping for justice involves the future anterior tense of the verb "to arrive." Injustice is bad however it arrives. But a justice that is hoped-for is not good unless it *will have arrived* through just means.

Even if legal coercion and justice do happen to stand apart at any given moment of history beneath the triangle's apex, hope wants – and all too often supposes – them to be more-or-less always vectoring in the same direction. Hope yearns for the ultimate arrival of a temporally distant point where law's force and the hoper's concept of justice finally intersect and are in complete harmony. At that point, a collective state of affairs that would be real **Justice** as such (and not merely its concept) hopefully will have arrived by just means. Along the way, it is the individual Self, and only the individual Self, who in each particular case must bear the burden of maintaining or upholding the law in a manner that is morally upright.

The rest of this chapter gives a critique of the foregoing customary interpretation of the relations amongst law, justice, and ethics. No magical potion or incantation can prevent human actions from setting off countless vibrations, large and small, in a world like ours that is subject to what Max Weber called the "infinite causal web" (1949: 84). The legal system, like sociology and historiography, is wont to assign responsibility for effects to causes, but only because it has particular "causal *interests* at the time" (1949: 178–79 n.38). Although those interests must be set into motion by individuals acting in the present, they are also codetermined by history, in the form of "the evaluative ideas which dominate the investigator and his age" (Weber, 1949:

Ethical doubts about justice 69

84). And as we saw in Chapter 3, the ways in which individuals ongoingly receive of these "evaluative ideas" (*Oughts*) are determined in large measure by custom (an *Is*). The ideas precondition lawyers, as they do sociologists and historians, to notice just *this* kind of phenomenon (a person's death, say) as "the effect" and *that* kind of phenomenon (a disease or act of homicide) as "the cause." Other candidates for causal analysis, other *Is*'s (say, systemic racial disparities in health and economic opportunity), fall by the wayside as irrelevant remainders cast off by the dominant causal account.

The force of law

The law is to justice and injustice as fire is to warmth and conflagration. That is, both history and experience teach that law can be used as a means to two contradictory ends: justice *and* injustice. Sometimes it leads to both at the same time, as Pascal observed about the contradictory nature of killing in a war where both sides can sincerely claim to be waging a *justum bellum* (1941: 293). Knowing this, politicians sometimes invite us to erase the conceptual distinction between law and justice by equating the latter with the complex of institutional practices known as "the rule of law." That offer might very well be declined, however, by someone in the position of the justice-seeking man from the country in Kafka's iconic parable *Before the Law* (1983). For anyone who has ever tried to peer around the law's doorkeeper to discover answers to questions such as, "The rule of which laws, exactly, and why them instead of better ones?" and "The rule of law by whom, for whom, and against whom?" eventually learns that the *rule of law* itself will not answer them.

The rule of law is paradoxical from the standpoint of pain. On the one hand, law's decision to deny or withhold justice is itself an injustice that inflicts a fresh wound on the victim of the original injustice. Yet, on the other hand, the choice to enforce legal justice no matter what creates new conditions that often wound indiscriminately. The awful experiences of the two young sons of Julius and Ethel Rosenberg, innocent of the charges brought against their executed parents (Meeropol, 2003); family members of a murder victim who suffer painful feelings of emptiness when they realize that the execution of the perpetrator did not "bring back the victim" (Muller, 2016); rape survivors whose ghastly experiences inside the criminal justice system have caused them to rue the day they ever reported the crime (McCarthy-Jones, 2018); whistleblowers who can no longer find work in their industries because employers interpret their legitimate expressions of concern to regulators as evidence of a propensity for disloyalty (Higginbottom, 2017); the heavy costs to African American families and communities from the sort of mass incarceration that Michelle Alexander has called "The New Jim Crow" (2012), etc. There is no justice that does not

70 *Ethical doubts about justice*

also resemble injustice when *all* of its consequences are considered from *all* of the points of view occupied by *everyone* affected.

In sum, although people like to think that new law can overcome the injustices of old law, history teaches that the ideal of a better-justice-to-come always seems to shine more brightly in the shop window than it does at home, after purchase. Revolutionary justice armed, or "lawmaking violence" (*rechtserhaltende Gewalt*), as Walter Benjamin calls it, promises much in the way of creating or restoring a just world. It sweeps away old law and replaces it with new law that itself must now be preserved if post-revolutionary (true) justice is to be done. Somehow, though, the shiny new "law-preserving violence" (*rechtsetzende Gewalt*) of the legal order to which revolutionary justice itself gives birth somehow never manages to fulfill all of its parent's promises (Benjamin, 1978: 292). Heads still have to roll, nonconforming bodies and minds still have to be controlled, and enough bread to feed the people still has to be found. Rarely, if at all, does the enactment of justice through law bring absolute satisfaction.

The resulting breach of faith grows ever more apparent the longer the law's authority lasts. One likes to think that the storming of the Bastille did not have to lead to the Terror; nor the Declaration of Independence to the Fugitive Slave Act; nor the October revolution to Stalin's show trials and the gulags; nor the Civil Rights Act of 1964 to white, working class resentment against its enforcement. It is as if the reputations of law and justice are inversely related to their coercive powers: the greater the real power of law or justice to enforce itself through the credible threat of violence, the shabbier is its reputation for unqualified goodness; and conversely, the weaker its power to forcibly inflict real suffering on the unwilling, the greater is its esteem as a distant goal worth pursuing.

No thinker has better expressed what is most worrisome about the fraught relationship between law and justice than the great seventeenth-century polymath Blaise Pascal. He went right to the heart of the matter in the first paragraph of one of his most famous *Pensées* ("thoughts" or "ideas"):

> It is right that what is just should be obeyed; it is necessary that what is strongest should be obeyed. Justice without might is helpless; might without justice is tyrannical. Justice without might is gainsaid, because there are always offenders; might without justice is condemned. We must then combine justice and might [*la justice et la force*], and for this end make what is just strong, or what is strong just.

> (1941: 103)

On its face, this passage seems to make a virtue out of necessity by arguing that there is, and perhaps should be, a symbiotic link between justice and

Ethical doubts about justice 71

what is "strongest" (*le plus fort*), which Pascal defines as that which has the greatest ability to use force (*la force*, translated earlier as "might"). In French, as in English, the word *force* is ambiguous. It can refer to a capacity, the actual exercise of that capacity, or both. Armed police officers, for example, have plenty of force at their disposal; they also use force if and when they wield their truncheons or discharge their guns. Lying conceptually somewhere between having and using force is the threat of it, which brings the possibility of violence to the attention of force's imminent recipients by making them aware of its pending menace.

The law, like a gunslinger, at once *possesses*, *threatens*, and *uses* force, a fact that Pascal conveniently summarizes in another aphorism by saying that the laws of a country owe their universality to "the might [*la force*] which is in them" (1941: 103). This brutally honest conclusion – "because there are always offenders," after all – is echoed in the very words we use to discuss legal matters. Thus, we ask whether a given rule of behavior has the "*force* of law" and, if it does, whether and by what means the authorities actually "en*force*" it.

The most fundamental problem raised by Pascal's interpretation of justice is how to understand the relationship between the force of law, which seems tangible enough, and the apparent forcelessness and impotence of justice in the absence of law. For we have been taught to believe, with Pascal, that law (*la loi*) and justice (*la justice*) are complementary but ultimately different concepts, like warp and woof or, better still, form and substance. Pascal's remarks appear to bind force, law, and justice to one another in the same way that the base of the isosceles triangle in Figure 4.1 supports its legs: only when law equals justice and justice equals law will force be able to carry them both without generating an unjust lacuna in appropriate coercion and an unjust remainder of inappropriate coercion.

Unlike a gunslinger, the law, as the acknowledged offspring of political struggle, represents the kind of force that most people in society accept as legitimate, at least most of the time. To be blunt about it, the law possesses a jealously guarded monopoly over the legitimate use of violence in society, up to and including the forcible taking of human life. But since "the law" itself has no material body – no arms, no legs, not even a larynx – it must depend on real, living human beings to read, understand, and execute its commands. Thus, it transpires that legal force, including the credible threat to use it, is routinely exercised every day by officials of the state: police, judges, executioners, prison guards, border patrol agents, government inspectors, agency administrators, etc. The law also uses countless nonstate actors to do its bidding by privileging them to use force in special situations: bail bondsmen, repo men, bouncers in bars, guards at for-profit private prisons, landowners fortifying their property with razor wire,

72   *Ethical doubts about justice*

storeowners detaining customers suspected of theft, gun owners "standing their ground," and so forth.

These examples illustrate something we all know: the law *is* powerful because civil society has let it *give* power to certain human beings.

Now imagine one of today's typical "at-will" fast food workers: a single mother, say, who needs the job to support her family. One minute she is unhappily serving burgers and fries while ill with the flu because she fears dismissal if she misses another day of work, and the next minute she is imperiously hustling a nonpaying homeless person out of the restaurant. "Boy, that one sure smelled bad," she says laughingly to a coworker. The protean nature of law's effects is such that in the blink of an eye a single individual can easily morph from being law's relatively passive object, or victim, into cheerfully acting as its ruthless enforcer.

A horse that has been whipped need not always feel the lash to run faster when urged on by a rider with a crop in her hand. Likewise, any sufficiently critical analysis of law's power *vis-à-vis* the individual must resist over-stressing the aforementioned semantic distinction between the law's having force and using it. Even without direct, on-the-spot verbal commands and threats of punishment – or rather, *especially* in the absence of such commands and threats – customary mass compliance with existing legal constraints produces profound effects on the individual's perceptions of what is normal, proper, and realistically possible in her social environment.

Law's power leaves traces that are visible everywhere, not just in televised arrests and court proceedings, not just in "No Trespassing" signs declaring "Violators Will Be Prosecuted," but also in less obvious places, such as our very own thoughts and feelings. It is as if the law were capable of altering its own physical state, going from a solid to a gas and entering our bodies through our senses even if we have never once had to deal with the legal system directly. The nervousness we feel when cutting across someone else's land to get where we are going; the anxiety of "walking while black" in a heavily policed white suburb; the faith that we "own" the very clothes on our back and in our closet; the belief that a boss has the "right" to fire an employee who refuses to work overtime or submit to a drug test; the certainty that citizens like us belong here and "illegal immigrants" do not; the conviction that our children have "earned" their way into college exclusively by hard work and individual initiative, and not also because we raised them in an affluent, gated community where the schools are well-funded by taxes; the reluctance to report a rape because it's only a "he said/she said" situation; etc., etc., etc.

The force of law is administered by the rule of law. Together they produce discipline, which Weber defined as "the probability that by habituation a command will receive prompt and automatic obedience in stereotyped

Ethical doubts about justice 73

forms, on the part of a given group of persons" (1978: I 34). As Weber's definition suggests, legal normalcy does not arise from an ongoing series of individual choices to submit to law's power. Legal normalcy *perdures* as a prerational state of affairs. History has a way of hardening accumulated past (often long past) legal commands into a solid block of "just the way things are." The apparent stability of the legal order is maintained primarily through the resulting social discipline. Legally induced social discipline is why the poor do not feel entitled to take what they so desperately need, when they need it. It is also why billionaires feel reasonably comfortable hoarding what they have, even if they don't need it. In sum, the lurking presence, and ongoing historical effects, of the law – its manifold decisions and inclinations to apply force or withhold it – constrain and enable pretty much all that we do, as well as all that is done to us.

Justice's guardianship over law

Whatever else may be said about it, the word *law* names a power to use force that has become routinized by most people accepting it as "the law of the land." How, then, should we talk about justice, or more precisely, about the *power* of justice? Pascal's previously noted *Pensée* on the relationship between justice and force rightly suggests that justice seems weak when compared to the force of law, for to paraphrase Stalin's disdainful remark about the Pope, justice has no divisions. No one has a legal privilege to forcibly establish justice without reference to the law, or justice as such. Revolutionaries may defend their use of violence by appealing to justice, but they are criminals in the eyes of the law, if not popular opinion, unless and until they succeed in overthrowing the state and establishing a new legal regime.

Although justice can look rather wimpy standing next to the force of law, this does not mean that it always behaves like a 98-pound weakling. Everyday opinion, if pressed, would probably agree that the much-vaunted value of the rule of law does not mean that it is perfectly alright to be ruled by any old law, however inhumane and evil it may be. Pascal's assertion that justice without force is "helpless" (*impuissante*) overstates the disparity between the power of law, which has its official minions to call upon, and the power of popular conceptions of justice, which do not.

In a world where the justice of a given legal arrangement is widely contested, popular conceptions of justice and injustice are not in fact totally helpless. The latter unofficially inhabit the minds and hearts of individuals and groups that are always capable of looking beyond the sphere of law proper and agitating for incremental or radical change. Fervent calls for justice above and beyond the terms established by the current political and legal system have been the hallmark of nearly every attempted revolution in

74   *Ethical doubts about justice*

history, including most visibly the successful American, French, and Russian revolutions. Peaceful acts of civil disobedience (Gandhi, Rosa Parks, Martin Luther King), while somewhat less dramatic than a revolution, are by definition intended to be "illegal" attacks on unjust laws. In a similar vein, other forms of lawbreaking are designed to draw attention to unjust conditions in daily life that the existing legal regime tolerates or ignores: the famous sit-down strikes in 1936–37 by auto workers in Flint, Michigan, for example, and more recently, the *gilets jaunes* ("yellow vests") protests by rightwing populists in France, as well as certain well-publicized protests for racial justice following several well-publicized instances of police brutality against African Americans in the spring of 2020.

Thus, by dint of history, ideology, and common opinion, many or most people imagine and hope that somehow or other the idea of justice will vigilantly stand guard over the law – that it will offer to protect us against law's biases and excesses, or, at the very least, that it will rise up and reproach the law whenever it permits or encourages injustice. This is not to say that everyone agrees what the idea of justice is, or how to define it, or whether it is the same for everyone. What matters most, figuratively speaking, is the belief that the gossamer flag of justice waves *above* the coarser flag of the law.

In what social contexts might justice be heard to gainsay the law? Aristotle long ago identified two major areas of inquiry about the relationship between justice and law (1130^a14–1131^a9). The first examines the way that the law articulates, in general, *what* people's rights and duties are (*distributive justice*). This question is ultimately decided in the various institutions where legal rules and principles are first created and announced: primarily legislative bodies at all levels of government, but also administrative agencies and courts. The second kind of justice examines *how* the legal system enforces people's already-established rights and duties in particular cases (*corrective justice*). This task mostly rests in the hands of police, prosecutors, private litigants, and in the final analysis, judges.

The average person on the street (not to mention Aristotle himself) would probably agree with the general proposition that property owners have a secondary legal right to a remedy for infringement of their legally recognized primary property rights. If you steal my car, not only will you go to jail, but I can also mulct you in damages in a court of law. But of course the distinction between distributive and corrective justice becomes especially problematic in cases where an unjust distribution of rights and duties is enforced by a legal system whose day-to-day operations happen to satisfy all the relevant procedural criteria of corrective justice (impartiality, fairness, due process, etc.).

Although Aristotle himself delicately sidestepped this particular problem, Robert Cover's magisterial study of the willingness of northern antislavery

Ethical doubts about justice 75

judges to enforce the Fugitive Slave Act in antebellum America provides a useful case in point (1984). The routine enforcement of slaveowners' property rights in their slaves during that period was sanctioned by both the U.S. Constitution and federal law. Often an exceedingly brutal affair, the exercise of this sort of "corrective justice" in the context of what most people today would call distributive injustice makes it difficult for many to accept the thesis that adherence to the rule of law has an inherent moral value that is completely independent of its content.

The precise terms of justice's guardianship over the law have been much contested, to put it mildly, during the long history of Western jurisprudence. Some, following the lead of Augustine[1] and Aquinas,[2] believe that duly enacted human laws which do not conform to "right reason" (*recta ratio*) or "natural law" (*lex naturalis*) are not really laws at all. Sometimes these thinkers derive their authoritative über-norms from God's commandments. Other times they derive them from stipulations about human nature and speculations about how human beings would behave in certain situations, such as the so-called state of nature (e.g. Hobbes, 1914; Locke, 1939b; Rousseau, 1993b).

Most of those who reject classical natural law theory follow a path called "legal positivism," which was blazed, most notably, by the British legal philosophers John Austin[3] and H. L. A. Hart.[4] Positivists maintain that questions about the existence, meaning, and practical effects of human laws are completely independent from questions about their goodness or badness as measured by some extralegal standard, such as morality or justice. Still other thinkers – Lon Fuller[5] and Ronald Dworkin,[6] for instance – sort of mush natural law and legal positivism together in complex and interesting ways, thereby introducing a carefully limited inquiry into what the law *Ought* to be into the process of deciding whether or what it really *Is*.

All of this is interesting and important, as are many of the other variations on these themes that can be found in the work of mainstream legal theorists. Nevertheless, let's put them aside as irrelevant to the primary focus of the present inquiry. Here we care less about the precise terms of justice's guardianship over law than we do about the fact that just about everyone thinks that justice *is* law's ultimate guardian.

It is also extremely significant that no one ever denies the readily observable fact that the law yearns to be called just and hates being called unjust. Hypocrisy is the compliment that vice pays to virtue, according to one of Rochefoucauld's best-known aphorisms. Even manifestly unjust legal regimes, to the extent they are interested in prolonging their rule, aspire to be seen and talked about as just. Whether you are a positivist, a natural law theorist, somewhere in between, or somewhere else, you must also realize that the masses would begin to believe that the force of law is illegitimate

76 *Ethical doubts about justice*

if officials display too much contempt for public opinion about the law's rightness or wrongness. For down that road lies popular revolt if not revolution, existing law's bane, which uproots old legal relations only to plant new ones in their place.

The shabbiness of law compared to the wonderfulness of justice

As the case of successful revolution pointedly illustrates, particular laws and legal regimes come and go, but mass acquiescence in the authority of "the law" (i.e. *some* form of law and order) remains more-or-less constant. Justice, however feeble its practical powers may be at the moment, and however squeamish some of its proponents may feel at the prospect of shedding blood, is not completely unaware of the practical imperative to connect ends (justice) with the means of achieving it (force).

To put it more directly, justice is no pacifist. That is why ever since ancient times artistic renderings of the goddess of justice routinely show her carrying a weapon. Figure 4.2 below, for example, is a nineteenth-century sketch of a painted Attic red amphora from the sixth century BCE (Teubner, 1884: 1019). It is one of the West's earliest depictions of Dikē, the goddess of justice. In it, Dikē wields a mallet or club to beat down Adikia, the personified spirit (*daimona*) of injustice and wrongdoing, depicted here as an ugly barbarian crone with tattooed skin.

In most paintings and sculptures, especially modern ones, Lady Justice appears less overtly brutal than she does in this drawing. Still, she almost always carries a mighty sword in one of her hands, either raised up and ready to strike or lowered and ready to be raised. Iconography that portrays justice as poised to inflict violence, if needful for her ends, is hardly accidental, for it coincides with popular opinion. Justice is widely seen as a keeper or custodian, not of this or that particular legal rule or regime, but rather of the *authority* of law in general – represented by the weapon that Dikē holds – to achieve and maintain whatever awesomely right result justice requires.

Natural law asserts this guardianship directly. It requires those who make and enforce legal norms forthrightly to consider what justice demands when deciding what the law itself is. But the imperative of discovering whether law is right or wrong does not disappear simply because natural law's positivist critics declare that law's factuality is analytically separate from its moral value. The debate between natural law and legal positivism is not really about whether *Ought* should conquer *Is*, or vice versa. It's about where and when *Ought* belongs in relation to *Is*. Even the most dyed-in-the-wool legal positivist would allow that justice must *sometimes* step out of the shadows and play an indispensable sociolegal role *vis-à-vis* the existing legal order.

Ethical doubts about justice 77

Figure 4.2 Dike and Adikia (Justice and Injustice)
Source: Image: Greek Mythology Link, www.maicar.com

To begin with, legal positivism freely concedes that it is appropriate for various traditions and conceptions of justice to openly contend with one another in the political sphere, where legal rules are first created. Moreover, while positivism does banish considerations of extralegal justice from legal decision-making, especially court judgments, it stops well short of recommending that legal actors permanently check their moral sensibilities at the courthouse door. On the contrary, though legal positivism has removed justice and morality from the metaphysical ether of universal right reason's claimed authority over the law, it nonetheless takes care to reanimate these values in the consciences of individual decision-makers.

This became a highly visible aspect of legal positivism after the gross scandal of German jurisprudence during the Nazi era. Almost all German judges and lawyers were legal positivists then (see Paulson, 2006). According to the findings of modern historical research, under National Socialism

78   *Ethical doubts about justice*

"German judges (purged of Jewish and Social Democratic colleagues) accommodated their legal reasoning to Nazism, whether servilely, eagerly, or fervently" (Morris, 2016: 652). It would be hard to find a legal positivist these days who would not sympathize with H. L. A. Hart's diagnosis of this situation. Hart held that the obligation of fidelity to law was suspended under such circumstances, and that everyone (judges and lawyers included) would retain the inalienable moral right – and perhaps the moral duty – to protest, resign, or resist if and when commanded to follow a manifestly unjust course of action by a regime as iniquitous as Nazi Germany was (1958: 616–20). *Pace* positivism's most strident critics, apparently the positivistic slogan, "The law is the law, not morals," does not conceal an utterly immoral, unethical heart after all.

Attempting to define the idea of justice as such – justice cut loose from any context that might be informed by the question of how and where it is considered, and by whom – would seem to be a fool's errand. As the previously noted historical example of due process for slaveowners illustrates, the potentially unstable Aristotelian distinction between distributive and corrective justice suggests the unwisdom of trying to summarize justice's all-encompassing "content" (in the singular). For it turns out that the concept of justice has been sliced and diced, and its parts deconstructed and recombined, in countless different ways.

For example: John Locke described justice *formally*, as the protection of people's preexisting natural rights (1939b: 453–55); John Stuart Mill described it *pragmatically*, as something dependent on the advancement of overall wellbeing and happiness (1939: 928–48); Robert Nozick described it *procedurally*, as the enforcement of historically-established entitlements (1974: 150–82); John Rawls described it *hypothetically*, as the principles that self-interested rational individuals would choose if they found themselves behind a veil of ignorance (1971: 136–42); Karl Marx described it *substantively*, as a distribution that receives from each according to his ability, and gives to each according to his needs (1959: 119); Walter Benjamin described it *religiously*, as God's "divine violence" bringing an apocalyptic end to the implementation of all merely human ("mythical") forms of legal violence (1978: 296–300); Roberto Unger described it *critically*, as the inevitable collapse into indeterminacy of the analytic distinction between distributive and corrective justice (1983: 1–14); Jack Balkin described it *affectively*, as a transcendent yearning in the human heart for a better world (1998: 162); Jacques Derrida described it *paradoxically*, as a social imperative that cannot wait despite being constantly deferred and never actually arriving in the present (1990: 967–71) . . . and so on and so forth, seemingly *ad infinitum*.

But if it would be naïve to think that justice is a one-size-fits-all concept, then it would be equally naïve to think that the linguistic sign **Justice** does not emit an attractive, nod-your-head-if-you-like-it aura all on its own. That aura

Ethical doubts about justice 79

explains why the law always tries to present itself – in bar association paeans to the rule of law, for example – as a kind of allegory whose hidden meaning is justice. Indeed, howsoever justice itself may be described – formally, pragmatically, procedurally, hypothetically, substantively, religiously, critically, affectively, paradoxically, *or in any other way* – it seems that just about everybody wants to praise it for its capacity to guard, if only weakly, against the realization of humanity's worst tendencies. Although history shows that the law can be, and often is, an engine of injustice, justice itself must be resplendently wonderful: that seems to be the takeaway from most of the stories written about law's relationship to justice.

Most stories, but not all. If people generally believe in the mantra *justice is good because law can be bad*, then they also have grounds to believe, rather inconsistently, that *law is good because justice can be dangerous*. The next section explores the ethical consequences of this nascent contradiction in the context of what is called the "fidelity to law" problem: the question of whether we have a moral duty (an *Ought*) to obey the law just exactly as it *Is*.

The problem of fidelity to law in a relativistic age

Mantra One

Justice Is Good Because Law Can Be Bad

This is certainly the position taken by natural law, which treats law and justice like two decks of cards that should always be shuffled together and dealt as one, in the way that blackjack dealers sometimes do in Las Vegas. If the only question at stake were the choice of means to a universally accepted, unquestionably valid end (the convergence of law and justice, as in Figure 4.1), then it would make perfect sense to accede to the implicit axiology of Mantra One, according to which justice is to law as a noble aspiration is to its imperfect realization, or as heaven is to earth. Then it would just be a technical matter, albeit not a simple one, of determining which jurisprudential point of view – natural law, legal positivism, or some other theory – stands the best chance of making the law more just. But alas, that is not the only question at stake.

Mantra Two

Law Is Good Because Justice Can Be Dangerous

The dominant approach to legal decision-making in almost all jurisdictions these days is legal positivism, which insists on keeping the two

80 *Ethical doubts about justice*

decks of cards separate. Just law and unjust law: if properly enacted, their common pedigree entitles both of them to the moniker *law*, which implies, in turn, that both have somehow earned the right to be obeyed and enforced. Why? The hue and cry of "judicial activism," frequently deployed as an epithet to criticize judicial decisions disliked by those who raise it, is the political expression of the belief that citizens in a democracy have a right to be ruled by the law itself, and not by some fallible judge's quirky-looking interpretation of the law. For a while, the nineteenth-century English positivist Jeremy Bentham's well-known diatribes against the common law for being vastly inferior to written, statutory law provided a certain amount of intellectual cover for this belief (1970). Although twentieth-century philosophers of language, especially Wittgenstein, have shown it to be inconsistent with linguistic reality, the belief itself remains popular. Despite its philosophical naïveté, belief in the bogeyman of unbridled judicial activism still remains a political and emotional force to be reckoned with. At bottom, this belief is one of the weapons that a customary way of receiving normative language (often a dominant group's ordinary way of understanding, or Is_1) employs to suppress a different customary way of receiving the very same set of linguistic signs (often a subordinate group's alternative way of understanding, or Is_2).

Notwithstanding their willingness to tolerate the exercise of individual moral choice to disobey or resist law's commands in the most extreme cases, the positivistic defenders of the constellation of values associated with the concept *the rule of law* are generally inclined to favor Mantra Two over Mantra One. Their preference for Mantra Two comes out most visibly when the time comes to talk about the so-called fidelity to law problem.

The fidelity to law problem can arise in many different contexts, but for the sake of brevity, let's just say that it pops up most often in academic debates about whether citizens have a general moral duty to obey *all* the laws of the state, including even those they consider to be unjust. According to Lon Fuller, legal positivism "never gives any coherent meaning to the moral obligation of fidelity to law." He goes on to describe the "dilemma" of positivism this way:

> On the one hand, we have an amoral datum called law, which has the peculiar quality of creating a moral duty to obey it. On the other hand, we have a moral duty to do what we think is right and decent. When we are confronted by a statute we believe to be thoroughly evil, we have to choose between those two duties.

(1958: 656)

Ethical doubts about justice 81

Now, the proposition that there is a *legal* duty to obey the law is as obvious as it is banal – it is equivalent to the tautology that the law imposes duties that the law itself enforces. That is pretty much all that having a legal duty really means. But having a *moral* duty to act unjustly by obeying or enforcing an unjust law, or at least a law that will produce unjust results? – that sounds a lot like saying you owe it to your health to eat greasy French fries with your sprouts whenever both are on offer.

In his famous debate with H. L. A. Hart, in which the preceding quotation appears, Fuller tried to draw a distinction between different *areas* of law within a state that most people today would call immoral and unjust: once again, Germany during the period of Nazi control, 1933–45. Fuller distinguished between cases arising in juridical fields that experienced "the most serious deterioration in legal morality under Hitler" and cases arising in "the ordinary branches of private law," where, according to Fuller, "no comparable deterioration was to be observed." This argument implies that the distinction between "those areas of law where the ends of law were most odious by ordinary standards of decency [and] the morality of law itself was most flagrantly disregarded" (e.g. criminal law, administrative law) and "the ordinary branches of private law" (e.g. contracts, property, torts) would remove the ethical taint of Nazi immorality from at least *some* Germans who chose to follow what they took, in good faith, to be the positivistic ethical obligation of fidelity to law.

This obligation is supposed to maintain adherence to the rule of law in society by imposing a moral duty on individuals to obey the law just because it happens to be the law, even if the regime does happen to be gassing the mentally disabled and transporting people to concentration camps for the crime of being Jewish, or Communist, or Roma, or gay. To be fair, Fuller mentioned the possibility of distinguishing between German public law and private law in 1958, well before the critical legal studies movement had begun to deconstruct the public/private distinction in jurisprudence, and well before the true scale and scope of Nazism's crimes against humanity had been widely publicized. Still, one can't help wondering whether (and how) the value of fidelity to law should apply to the negotiation, drafting, and enforcement of the many "private" contracts of sale entered into between "Aryans" and impecunious Jewish businessmen desperate to raise funds to leave the country as soon as possible (see Hickley, 2020).

Pace Fuller, just about everyone these days, regardless of which jurisprudential school they belong to, would concede that there is no *general* moral obligation to obey or enforce the laws of what the Israeli legal philosopher Joseph Raz has called an "unjust state." "But it is contended there is an obligation to obey the law of a reasonably just state," Raz goes on to say,

82 *Ethical doubts about justice*

"and the greater its justice the stricter, or at any rate the clearer, the obligation" (1999: 160). Raz himself certainly never contended this, but other notable thinkers have. The Australian natural law philosopher John Finnis, for example, has argued that in a state that is "reasonably just" by his criteria – one where benefits and burdens are fairly and widely distributed for the common good – "law presents itself as a seamless web. Its subjects are not [morally?] permitted to pick and choose among the law's prescriptions and stipulations"(1984: 120).

The predicate for Finnis's assertion that there exists a general moral duty to obey the law is the ethical duty of loyalty. Everyone in a reasonably just state, he argues, has a duty of loyalty to the community that entails a subsidiary moral duty to adhere to whatever makes that community possible, including especially the rule of law. It is unclear, however, why anyone should have a general moral duty to *feel* loyal to a monolithic community (or pseudo-community) whose own government's laws are used to create injustice. The empirical existence of any individual feeling of belonging to such a community is clearly not a given, but rather is contingent on many factors. That is why Anatole France's best-known aphorism never fails to puncture the conceit behind the argument that obedience to the law is required by an individual duty of loyalty to what makes the so-called community possible: "The law, in its majestic equality, forbids the rich as well as the poor to sleep under the bridges, to beg in the streets, and to steal bread." Raz's response to Finnis's argument, though less biting than France's, rightly observes that the merely *possible* existence of such a feeling of belonging cannot supply the reason for a *general* moral duty, binding on everyone, to swallow the bitter (unjust laws) with the sweet (just laws) (1999: 160).

The particular Raz/Finnis debate that we have been discussing did not explicitly address the moral duties of lawyers and judges *vis-à-vis* the enforcement of unjust laws. But in refuting Finnis's argument that there is a general moral duty to obey the laws of a reasonably just state, Raz, one of the most prominent legal positivists writing today, introduces the possibility that there might be a role for individual ethicality in the legal system that goes beyond, and may even contradict, the everyday duties that are imposed on legal actors by their official codes of professional conduct.

It is sometimes said that the act of explicitly consenting to be governed by the law's commands – as judges and other officials do when they take their oaths of office – can provide an independent moral reason to enforce a law that the consent-giver now thinks is either unjust on its face or as applied to a particular situation. Article VI of the U.S. Constitution, for example, requires state officials, including state judges, to "be bound by oath or affirmation, to support this Constitution." One very big problem with deducing from this clause the proposition that judges have a moral duty to apply the

Ethical doubts about justice 83

Constitution in a way that produces injustice in a particular case is that the meaning of the judicial oath is itself hotly contested (see Balkin, 2020). Do the words "this Constitution" in the oath refer to the Constitution as understood by the Framers in 1789? To the Constitution as currently interpreted by the Supreme Court? To the very best interpretation of the Constitution that the oath-taker can give despite what others may have said about it? To the Constitution as an ongoing legal and political institution that says nothing about how it should be interpreted?

If the meaning of the oath of office is unsettled, then the oath itself cannot be more binding, morally speaking, than any of its good faith interpretations would allow the oath-taker to make. Not only that, it seems to be a huge logical leap, to say the least, to go from a moral commitment to fairly apply the rules of procedural justice to the Constitution to a moral duty to enforce any substantive outcome, no matter how disgusting, so long as it was fairly produced.

Real injustice, like real suffering, is never abstract, but always painfully concrete. It is a hard thing indeed to come face to face with someone whose legal fate not only strikes you as morally wrong, but also depends on your own actions as a lawyer or judge to bring about. To superimpose a distinctly *moral* obligation on top of a merely *legal* duty to enforce the law in such a case does not just seem paradoxical, as Lon Fuller noted. It also verges on being what Raz calls a "moral perversion" (1999: 161).

During the Middle Ages – the heyday of natural law thinking in Europe – the Church taught, or at least tried to teach, everyone to believe in the same set of moral values. The concept of justice was officially **Justice** (capitalized and in the singular). If there was optimism, it was because people were told that the world is good and beautiful just as it is, as Leibniz did when he praised God's creation as the best of all possible worlds (2017: 156). It was just this sort of claimed universal duty of optimism that Marx criticized when he wrote, in 1843, that religion is the opium of the people.[7]

After the Reformation, however, and especially in the decades and centuries following the European Enlightenment, the individual's own conscience was emancipated from traditional ties of religious orthodoxy and uniformity. It's not so much that God died, as Nietzsche famously asserted (1961: 41). It's that belief in God and the justice of his ordinances eventually became completely optional for the individual. You and your God may think it is morally wrong for me to covet my neighbor's maidservant, ox, or ass (Exodus 20:17), but I disagree and consider it good for the economy. Who are you to say I cannot model my own consumerism on yours? With the rise of the secular state, voluntary adherence by individuals and groups to this or that moral creed, this or that interpretation of justice, replaced mandatory adherence to a single creed enforced by social custom and sovereign law.

84   *Ethical doubts about justice*

Leibniz's sort of optimism is long gone. If today there is a "new optimism," as George Patrick's eponymous popular essay put it a century ago (ironically, right before the outbreak World War I), it is because individuals believe they can *make* the world good and beautiful, not because it already is (1913).

It is little wonder, then, that by the end of the nineteenth century the then-ascendant theory of legal positivism could take it for granted that the existence and contents of legal norms are completely separable from the individual's own moral choices *vis-à-vis* the enforcement of those norms. At some point in world history, after a long period of decline, justice ceased being **Justice**, just as God ceased being the only possible god when freedom of religion in the modern secular nation state eventually made belief in any one version of Him/Her/It optional. It is as if the statue of the goddess Dikē were miniaturized and reproduced on a vast scale, fragmenting the big concept of **Justice** into a plethora of unofficial, different, and inconsistent little justice*s*, each one suitable for installation in the secular prayer nooks of individuals, families, and factions. If the iconic Goddess of Justice that stands on plinths in front of so many courthouses around the world could lift her blindfold to see how ill-used she has become, she would weep.[8]

"The fate of our times is characterized by rationalization and intellectualization and, above all, by the disenchantment of the world," said Max Weber, adding that "the ultimate and most sublime values have retreated from public life either into the transcendental realm of mystic life or into the brotherliness of direct and personal human relations" (1958: 155). In a disenchanted world, neither natural law nor legal positivism can plausibly claim to impose an official dogma that is both legally and morally binding *a priori* on every individual. Their common premise is that the idea, or feeling, or. . . *whatever*, of justice at the very minimum gives each *individual person*, in advance, a rational or emotive criterion to evaluate and criticize the law. Once the individual finds and applies this criterion, both schools of jurisprudence hope that certain beneficial real effects will follow. These might take the form of judicial interpretations or judicial resignations, legislative reforms or acts of courageous resistance. But whatever form these good results take, they all come down to being real, palpable effects of how the linguistic sign "justice" is actually received by individual actors in each new case.

"An unjust law," said Aquinas "has the nature, not of law, but of violence" (1940: 633). But categorical denials, like explicit moral prohibitions, sometimes betray an unconscious desire to transgress their boundaries. In Aquinas's presupposition that just laws, were they ever to exist, do *not* have the nature of violence lies a clue to the secretly reciprocal relationship between law and justice. For his subsequent defense of the justice of "natural slavery" and the obvious legal coercion that it entails demonstrates

Ethical doubts about justice 85

the untenability of the thesis that just law is a stranger to force.[9] Here, as elsewhere, the idea of justice gives law its potential legitimacy at the very same time that the idea of law gives justice a coveted means to achieve its ends. In one way or another, Aquinas, Pascal, and our own Axiom of Legal Progress all affirm the unquestionable goodness of the same tautology: *Just Legal Force↔Justice Legalized.*

Our earlier investigations into the mutually constitutive relationship between *Is* and *Ought* suggest that the power of justice's currently operative ideas and images, like those of law, are both outside us *and* inside us. But the view that the ethical enforcement of just law presents absolutely no moral problem at all – a corollary of the Axiom of Legal Progress – is the functional equivalent of saying that if anyone is condemned by the dominant ideas and images of the justice that is inside us, then they deserve to suffer. The oppression or annihilation of naysayers and deviants is a feature of the Axiom, not a bug. The Axiom can therefore be seen as the secular equivalent of Aquinas's sadistic thesis that the souls of the saved in heaven will be able to enjoy their blissful state even more by watching the torments of the damned in hell.[10]

The customary agreeableness of justice

"As custom determines what is agreeable," said Pascal in yet another *Pensée*, "so also does it determine justice" (1941: 105). The thesis is that justice gets its bearings not from a holy book, not from right reason, indeed not from anywhere else than customary ways of thinking and talking. In the amphora drawing shown in Figure 4.2, for example, it is no accident that the classically Greek-looking goddess Dikē is shown assaulting an Adikia depicted as an ugly, tattooed, barbarian woman. Aristotle, clearly reflecting the prejudices of his time, approvingly quoted the poets as saying, "It is meet that Hellenes should rule over barbarians," adding, "as if they thought that the barbarian and the slave were by nature one" (1252^b5-9). If the sense of injustice is determined in large measure by what people like Aristotle take for granted as normal, then the mere maintenance or restoration of normalcy as such – including all of its unquestioned and unquestionable social hierarchies – will automatically count as a triumph of justice.

The close connection between justice and law's legitimate use of force thus reflects and reinforces the close connection between justice and custom. And this connection, in turn, includes the special but hardly unusual case of intercultural conflicts about different customary ways of thinking and being.

Consider, as a prime example of the latter, the violent ideological conflict between slavery and abolitionism that ultimately led to the American Civil War. President Abraham Lincoln drew on the same sort of militant imagery

86 *Ethical doubts about justice*

that is shown in Figure 4.2's depiction of Dikē/justice clubbing Adikia/ injustice when, during his second inaugural address, he stirringly intoned:

> If God wills that [the war] continue until all the wealth piled by the bondsman's two hundred and fifty years of unrequited toil shall be sunk, and until every drop of blood drawn with the lash shall be paid by another drawn with the sword, as was said three thousand years ago, so still it must be said "the judgments of the Lord are true and righteous altogether."
>
> (1865)

Lincoln's reference to the absolute righteousness of God's judgments is telling. The logic of his argument transforms what *Is* (a war that the North by that time was winning) into what *Ought* to be (the destruction of slavery) just by virtue of its having happened at all (*Is→Ought*). His rhetoric therefore skillfully elides the ironic Pascalian distinction between making what is just strong and what is strong just.

At the time, Lincoln's words about the justice of ending slavery and maintaining the Union was a much-iterated theme in the Northern press. It was often written about, yes, but it was also not uncontroversial. Protestors during the violent 1863 New York City draft riots, for example, had shouted, "It's a rich man's war and a poor man's fight" after the enactment of a "universal" conscription law that allowed inductees to buy their way out of military service by paying $300 to the government. Members of the Democratic Party's peace wing (the "Copperheads") had denounced the law as an unjust burden on the white working class, most of whom lacked the financial resources necessary to avoid the draft.

Sure enough, the protests quickly turned into violent race riots in which white mobs hunted down and lynched over a hundred African Americans (Schechter, 2007). Following the riots, the magazine *Harper's Weekly* printed several political cartoons illustrating them, including the one shown in Figure 4.3 by an unknown artist.

Look closely at this image. Its visual similarity to Dikē beating Adikia with a club in Figure 4.2 below is undeniable. Ideas of justice, it would seem, always need *some* Other to overcome and bludgeon. If not a tattooed barbarian, then an old black man and the child he protects. And if not them, then the club wielding draft rioters themselves, whom the anonymous cartoonist so obviously condemns ("beats") with pen and ink. For clubs and swords are not the only weapons in Dikē's arsenal; she has been known to deploy violence-inducing words and images, too.

The example of the New York City draft riots is an uncomfortable reminder of the familiar old academic claim that all of our conceptions of justice are historically, culturally, and factionally relative, not universal. And it is a fact that rational "moral" principles supporting slavery, scientific

Ethical doubts about justice 87

Figure 4.3 "How to Escape the Draft"[11]

racism, colonial expropriations, patriarchy, and genocidal policies against the Other have all had their vociferous religious and secular defenders.

- Saint Augustine said slavery is a just punishment for sin (*City of God* 19:15).
- Thomas Jefferson, author of the Declaration of Independence, wrote that "blacks, whether originally a distinct race, or made distinct by time and circumstances, are inferior to the whites in the endowments both of body and mind" (1999: 150–51).
- Pope Alexander VI blessed European colonization of Africa and the New World by issuing a papal bull in 1493 commanding that "barbarous nations be overthrown and brought to the faith" (Gallagher, 2018).
- Women should not have the right to practice law, wrote Supreme Court Justice Joseph Bradley in 1872, because "The paramount destiny and mission of woman are to fulfil the noble and benign offices of wife and mother" (Bradwell, 1872: 141).
- The *Berliner Tageblatt*, a Weimar-era newspaper, justified the mass slaughter of Armenians by the Turkish government by arguing, "This is the price for treason!" (Ihrig, 2016: 297).

88   *Ethical doubts about justice*

- Testifying in 1937 about the problem of unrest in the British Mandate of Palestine, Winston Churchill said: "I do not admit that a great wrong has been done to [the aboriginal peoples of America and Australia] by the fact that a stronger race, a higher grade race, or, at any rate, a more worldly-wise race, to put it that way, has come to take their place" (Mount, 2019: 22).

We could go on and on quoting rational defenses of practices that are now widely considered to be morally indefensible. But the main thing to notice about these and other examples is not their epistemological defects, which are many, but rather what their psycho-ethical effects on the individual were at the time. The arguments in these defenses were either consciously believed or taken for granted by most of those who benefitted from the practices in question, not to mention (sadly enough) by many of those whom the principles affirmatively disadvantaged and who might have had the most to gain from contesting them.[12]

Ever since Marx's day, the unflattering name that modern social science, whether Marxist or non-Marxist, has bestowed on an era's taken-for-granted dictates of faith and reason is "ideology." This oft-quoted passage from the sociologist Karl Mannheim's *Ideology and Utopia* summarizes the general social function that ideology performs:

> The concept "ideology" reflects the one discovery which emerged from political conflict, namely, that ruling groups can in their thinking become so intensively interest-bound to a situation that they are simply no longer able to see certain facts which would undermine their sense of domination. There is implicit in the word "ideology" the insight that in certain situations the collective unconscious of certain groups obscures the real condition of society both to itself and to others and thereby stabilizes it.
>
> (1985: 40)

The nagging worry that today's seemingly hidebound moral truths can and will someday be interpreted as ideological in Mannheim's sense poses, or should pose, a grave challenge to critical thought about ethics in relation to law.

So, shall we say that cultural relativism is true, and universalism false? The answer we give here is that neither one is true *and* neither one is false, for to apply the binary true/false to this question would be a category mistake. Inasmuch as absolute universalism and absolute relativism are both immune to any counterevidence that their proponents could not appropriate for their own purposes – flip, so to speak – by marshalling the one-sided stipulations of their own metaphysical systems, it would be pointless to try to prove the "truth" or the "falsity" of either of them (cf. Kant's antinomies of

Ethical doubts about justice 89

pure reason). As is the case with the antithesis between religion and atheism, the choice between universalism and relativism is at bottom ethical and rhetorical, not metaphysical or empirical. Universalism says, "Trust my instincts about justice because they are based on universal value X." Relativism says, "Never trust *any* claim that is articulated in universal terms." But when seen from the point of view of an ethics writ large, the essence of what both of them invite us to do is just this: "Close your eyes, hold my hand, and leap!"

Instead of being offered as some kind of proof, the juxtaposition of Figures 4.2 and 4.3 at this point in our investigations has a more limited purpose. It is meant to show only that things can get quite ugly, quite fast when justice for *some* begins to show itself to *others* as unjust legal force. For just as there can be a widespread longing in the oppressed and their friends for today's legal order to be made more just, so too there is such a thing as the nostalgia of formerly privileged groups for a bygone era whose legal arrangements were swept away by the political success of some other group's conception of justice. "Make America Great Again" indeed! In the same way that the excitement of anticipation is replaced by the ho-hummery of possession, history teaches that the very moment the ideals of justice become law they begin to tarnish. For that is when the direct and collateral costs of their enforcement through violence and the threat of violence – law's "suppression of hostile counter-violence," as Benjamin puts it (1978: 300) – start to pile up.

It is sometimes said that people can identify injustice, and say why it is unjust, better than they can identify or describe justice as such (see, e.g., Shklar, 1990: 15–16). This may explain why the philosopher Amartya Sen, in his excellent book *The Idea of Justice*, makes popular feelings and perceptions of *injustice* rather than justice into the "starting point" for his theory of justice (2009: VII-VIII). Pindar's poem *The Power of Custom*, quoted as an epigram to Chapter 2, suggests why this sort of argument is able to generate considerable emotional appeal. The everyday social life of most people rests on the feather (or concrete) pillow of what they take for granted as "normal." Thus, we tend to notice and condemn hurtful outcomes that deviate from the *Is* of normalcy – *whatever* it may be – more readily than we do when the hurtfulness has become socially routinized and generalized over a long period of time.

The *normalcy-is-good-and-not-unjust* bias explains why there were few if any public protests against the use of blackface scenes in Irving Berlin's patriotic Christmas musical *Holiday Inn*, when the movie was first released in 1942. On the contrary, critics lauded the film for its "lighthearted and affectionate spirit," and praised its star, Bing Crosby, for his casual ability to "sell a blackface song like 'Abraham' or turn an ordinary line into sly humor without seeming to try" (Strauss, 1942). The fact that times have

90 *Ethical doubts about justice*

changed and that the use of blackface in motion pictures today is widely condemned as unjust and immoral, shows that customs can change. But the changeability of customs over time does not make them any less powerful, or less hurtful, during the time they *do* hold sway. In its proper season the customary shows itself to most people, including the proponents of ethics writ small, as a neutral growth medium, not a virus.

Theories of justice like Sen's are double-edged swords. On the one hand, they can jolt us out of unthinkingly accepting what is taken for granted as the only measure of what is just or unjust – and this is undoubtedly a good thing. But on the other hand, they are still *discourses* that present themselves as being immune from customary ways of receiving them – and this can be a bad thing. If faithfully following Sen's or anyone else's rational theory of justice to the very end leads one to conclude, in any given situation, that the infliction of legal suffering on this or that particular person is "just," or at least "not unjust," then this is just another way of conveying the psychologically deep-seated message of the Axiom of Legal Progress: **The ethically correct enforcement of just law is always good and desirable.**

The suspicious wordiness of reason

Your author will henceforth speak to you in the first person. What is at stake in this book is too important for me to hide any longer under the grammatical carapace of faux authorial objectivity. Ever since Nietzsche's *Beyond Good and Evil*, if not before, everyone knows (or should know) that at the end of the day a work of philosophy, whether it be great or otherwise, is always a covert autobiography anyway.[13]

I used to swallow the dogma embedded in the Axiom of Legal Progress whole. Who but a miscreant, I thought, could be against making the world a better, more just place? Eventually, though, the thesis that the ethically correct enforcement of just law is never a problem started to stick in my craw. It seemed to place too much reliance on the power of reason, fueled as it is by a superstitious belief in the quasi-magical powers of language, to assuage individual feelings of guilt and personal responsibility. I knew that in *The Social Construction of Reality*, an influential treatise on the sociology of knowledge, Peter Berger and Thomas Luckmann had argued, rather convincingly, I thought, that (1) "No 'history of ideas' takes place in isolation from the blood and sweat of general history," and (2) "all symbolic universes and all legitimations are human products [whose] existence has its base in the lives of concrete individuals and has no empirical status apart from these lives" (1967: 128).

The dual insight that law, justice, and ethics all create symbolic universes that would be nothing at all without individuals to sustain them was like

Ethical doubts about justice 91

a flashlight in the dark. It pitilessly illuminated what Levinas was one of the first to notice: namely, that there is something truly terrible about the cruelties that "proceed from the necessity of the reasonable Order." These are the cruelties, I saw now, that individuals keep on tolerating or ignoring, like well-trained mules in harness, "even when the hierarchy functions perfectly, when everyone submits to universal ideas" (1996: 23). For those who want to move with the times are not allowed – or rather, do not allow themselves – to be different (cf. Adorno, 2005: 139).

After reading Levinas, I began to think that ethics interpreted as a rationally inscrutable but unavoidable personal burden carried for the sake of others – *all* others – could and should stand guard over whatever image of normalcy and/or concept of justice one happens to believe in. What if, contrary to the apparent message of Pascal's *Pensée*, the human heart contained too little primordial, prerational individual guilt on account of *both* might *and* justice, including any conceivable program aimed at coordinating them?

The historically delivered concepts that we associate with the linguistic sign **Justice** are like tinted spectacles on a severely myopic person. Having been led by history and fate to receive (and not just understand) these concepts in the way that we do, they are what allow us even to notice the moral dimension of social arrangements in the first place. But the flip side of any concept – and maybe even its only side – is its expression in words-as-received, and they can be treacherous things. No concept can apply itself to reality, and when put into practice in countless concrete situations, no concept of justice, however noble sounding, is immune to malign historical influences.

The Manichaean tendency to become obsessively attached, in any given situation, to squeezing reality into one side or the other of a pair of dualistic images and symbols – in this case, justice versus injustice – can create a paradoxical situation in which an increase in justice actually produces an increase (not a decrease) in injustice. "A problem with our 2500 years of programmatic justice theorists," writes legal philosopher Eric Heinze, "is that they see injustice as an accident or a privation, and not as a substantive product of justice as *they* conceive it" (2013: 9). Having attended countless academic conferences, I can report that even the hipster's claim that the concept of justice is always culturally relative is more often than not grounded in individual certainty about the non-relativism of the hipster's own most cherished beliefs. And so: "Wretchedness remains. When all is said,/It cannot be uprooted, live or dead./So it is made invisible instead" (Adorno, 2005: 59).

This helps to explain why the second paragraph of Pascal's *Pensée* no. 298, the first paragraph of which was quoted earlier in this chapter, strikes a

92 *Ethical doubts about justice*

tone that is decidedly less optimistic and more ironic than the first about the prospect of eventually harmonizing law with justice.

> Justice is subject to dispute; might is easily recognized and is not disputed. So, we cannot give might to justice, because might has gainsaid justice, and has declared that it is she herself who is just. And thus, being unable to make what is just strong, we have made what is strong just.
>
> (1941: 103)

In his account of the siege of Melos during the Peloponnesian war, Thucydides recounts that the emissaries from the invading Athenians bluntly told the much-weaker Melians that "the strong do what they can, and the weak suffer what they must" (1961: 359). This rhetorical strategy is the exception, however, not the rule. History teaches that the strong hardly ever undertake to dominate the weak without giving them any credible explanation besides their raw power to do so. The legal arrangements of the victorious and the strong usually seduce the defeated and the weak into submission in the name, not of force alone, but of said force's superior *rightness* and *justice*. Like *Arbeit Macht Frei*, these two linguistic signs somehow emit a benign aura no matter what deeds and programs they are being used to underwrite.

That is why the legend chiseled into the front façade of the U.S. Supreme Court building in Washington, D.C., does not read "Equal Force under Law," nor even "Equal Law under Law," but rather "Equal Justice under Law." I confess that, well before the turn of the millennium, the latter slogan began to look more like a superstitious talisman to me than it did the rational expression of a noble aspiration. Nothing that has happened since then has lessened this impression.

Nietzsche once said, plausibly enough, that the real opinions of philosophers may pose as cold, hard truths, but in reality are "generally their heart's desire abstracted and refined" (1954: 385). But this book is not offered as an argument against the desire and hope for justice, nor against collective efforts to seek justice through law and politics. Such an argument would be futile anyway, since the twin psychological phenomena of hope and disappointment are probably just as much anthropological necessities as the need to eat and breathe. The book has, however, challenged and attempted to refute the conventional claim that the role of individual ethics in relation to law and justice is limited to resisting unjust law and advancing the goals of just law in a fair manner.

Both law and justice are collective enterprises – they speak about *Us* and *Them*. If law needs justice as its guardian, then it seems to me that justice needs its own guardian, lest it become a monstrous machine whose gears and cogs happen to be you and me. In an ethics writ large, there is only one possible candidate for who should become this guardian. In every individual case this guardian could only be a particular *Me-Myself* trying to respond with decency to a particular *Thou*, and with respect to all the other *Thou*'s, in an ethical present that is, in a manner of speaking, carrying unborn twins within itself: reason *and* compassion.

Notes

1 "[T]here is nothing just and lawful in temporal law that human beings have not derived from eternal law" (Augustine, 1994: 216–17).
2 "Human law has the nature of law in so far as it partakes of right reason; and it is clear that it is derived from the eternal law [of God]. But in so far as it deviates from reason, it is called an unjust law, and has the nature, not of law, but of violence" (Aquinas, 1940: 632-33).
3 "The existence of law is one thing; its merit and demerit another. Whether it be or be not is one enquiry; whether it be or be not conformable to an assumed standard, is a different enquiry" (Austin, 1998: 132–33).
4 "[T]heories that make this close assimilation of law to morality seem, in the end, often to confuse one kind of obligatory conduct with another, and to leave insufficient room for differences in kind between legal and moral rules and for divergences in their requirements" (Hart, 1961: 7–8).
5 "[W]e may speak of a procedural, as distinguished from a substantive natural law. . . . The term 'procedural' [indicates] that we are concerned, not with the substantive aims of legal rules, but with the ways in which a system of rules for governing human conduct must be constructed and administered if it is to be efficacious and at the same time remain what it purports to be" (Fuller, 1969: 97).
6 "Law's empire is defined by attitude, not territory or power or process. . . . Law's attitude is constructive: it aims, in the interpretive spirit, to lay principle over practice to show the best route to a better future, keeping the right faith with the past" (Dworkin, 1986: 413).
7 "Religion is the sigh of the oppressed creature, the heart of a heartless world, just as it is the spirit of an unspiritual situation. It is the opium of the people" (Marx, 1959: 263).
8 Dikē's statuette has shrunk so much that the neo-Nazi website *Stormfront* could cynically, yet shrewdly and effectively, appropriate the language of justice "to echo the way African-Americans, Latinos, and women talked about their experience of oppression" in order to "protect and preserve an endangered heritage and culture [of whites from] inevitable genocide by mass immigration and mass assimilation" (Hochschild, 2019: 72).
9 "Since slavery was imposed in punishment of sin, it follows that by slavery man forfeits something which otherwise would belong to him, namely the free disposal of his person, for a slave, as regards what he is, belongs to his master" (*Summa Theologica*, II-II, q.189, a.6, arg.2).
10 *Beati in regno celesti videbunt poenas damnatorum, ut beatudo illis magis complaceat,* said Aquinas: "The souls in heaven will be able to enjoy the blissfulness of paradise all the more because they can view the torment of the damned in hell" (Heidegger & Fink, 1993: 125).
11 Political cartoon, *Harper's Weekly*, August 1, 1863, artist unknown. From *Wikimedia Commons*. Available at: https://commons.wikimedia.org/wiki/File:Harpers_Weekly_cartoon_-_escape_draft.jpg

94 *Ethical doubts about justice*

12 See Antonio Gramsci's well-known analysis of the society-wide "hegemony" of ruling class ideas (1971: 161).

13 "It has gradually become clear to me what every great philosophy up till now has consisted of – namely, the confession of its originator, and a species of involuntary and unconscious autobiography; and moreover that the moral (or immoral) purpose in every philosophy has constituted the true vital germ out of which the entire plant has always grown" (Nietzsche, 1954: 386).

5 A concluding anecdote about the difference between ambiguity and treachery

> The main business of a lawyer is to take the romance, the mystery, the irony, the ambiguity out of everything he touches.
>
> Antonin Scalia (2005)

> Ambiguity is the manifest imaging of the dialectic, the law of dialectics at a standstill.
>
> Walter Benjamin (1999: 10)

"But this *is* a pipe": a law professor's anecdote

Some of the unorthodox thoughts discussed in this book were on my mind when, after sitting through yet another tedious faculty meeting sometime in the early 1990s, I made a spur-of-the-moment decision to initiate a brief discussion about the ethics of law and justice with the distinguished older law school professor sitting next to me. Maybe the devil made me do it, for he was not exactly a friend of mine, and in fact had always seemed to treat me with a certain amount of reserved indifference. In retrospect, I see now that I probably deserved the indifference, but at the time I thought that this moment might present a good opportunity to try sparking some sort of intellectual connection between us.

Reaching into my briefcase, I brought out a photocopy of René Magritte's iconic painting *La Trahison des images* ("The Treachery of Images," Figure 5.1). I happened to have a copy with me because I was contemplating using it as an illustration for a paper I was researching at the time. I had the vague idea that the paper would examine the ethical (and not just juridical) connection between an individual's official use of legal language – statutes, case law, legal judgments, judicial opinions, attorneys' arguments, etc. – and the often-tragic human reality that the legal system as a whole both supervises and reproduces.

96 *Difference between ambiguity and treachery*

Figure 5.1 La Trahison des images ("The Treachery of Images")[1]

Since my colleague understood French, he had no difficulty immediately translating *Ceci n'est pas une pipe* as "This is not a pipe." After staring at the picture for quite a while, at last he piped up: "But it *is* a pipe," he exclaimed. "I don't get it." My colleague was not a stupid man. In truth he was very smart. Politically conservative, he was the kind of person who liked to celebrate the American Bar Association's panegyrics to the rule of law on "Law Day," which rolls around once every year on May 1st. I had also heard him say, in informal faculty discussions, that critical legal theory and, I suppose, people like me who wasted their time doing it, had very little of value to contribute to the study of the law. Since Magritte is one of those artists who hoped that his work would be philosophically thought-provoking and not just aesthetically stimulating, I tried to get through to my colleague by quoting what the painter himself had said about those who remain unable or unwilling to grasp what "The Treachery of Images" is getting at:

> The famous pipe. How people reproached me for it! And yet, could you stuff my pipe? No, it's just a representation, is it not? So, if I had written on my picture "This is a pipe," I'd have been lying!
> (Torczyner, 1977: 71)

It seemed pretty clear to me that Magritte's remark was making the basic point that a painted image of a pipe is not the same thing, or even the same kind of thing, as a real pipe. Nevertheless, hearing me read Magritte's response to his critics out loud made no difference to my colleague. Apparently, I had awakened his competitive-argumentative spirits – an easy thing to do with law professors – for he proceeded to poke his finger onto the paper-and-ink

Difference between ambiguity and treachery 97

image lying on the desk in front of us and announce, with barely disguised annoyance, "You'll never convince me that *this* is not a pipe." And on that note the conversation ended, and we returned alone to our respective offices.

The indeterminacy thesis

Looking back on this incident after more than a quarter century, now that I myself have become an old[er] law professor, I believe that my colleague's reaction to Magritte's painting was probably motivated by suspicion about my intellectual motives. I believe he thought that I was somehow trying to trick him into agreeing with the notorious "indeterminacy thesis," which at that time still remained a hot topic for discussion in law school faculty lounges. Members of the emerging Critical Legal Studies (CLS) movement had written quite a few law review articles and books in the 1970s and '80s attempting to demonstrate that even the clearest legal rules and principles could, given the right factual circumstances, be reasonably interpreted to mean something other than what settled legal opinion and common understanding took them to mean (see, e.g., Gabel, 1984; Kairys, 1990; Kelman, 1987; Kennedy, 1976; Unger, 1983).

Many decades earlier, in the 1920s and '30s, the proponents of American Legal Realism had shown, in many different areas of law, that legal rules and principles are essentially *multivocal*: that is, capable of producing two or more inconsistent, but nonetheless rationally defensible, results in particular cases (see generally Fisher, Horwitz, & Reed, 1993). CLS had rediscovered these old books and articles, and, with the assistance of a hodgepodge of insights drawn from the Marxist tradition and from postmodern philosophy, psychology, and literary theory, had greatly expanded the scope of the realists' work. CLS scholars in America had expressed the indeterminacy thesis in many different ways in the period between the late 1970s and early '90s, and their liberal and conservative critics in academia had launched vociferous counterattacks, both on the thesis itself as the critics interpreted it (Dworkin, 1986: 271–74; Solum, 1987) and on the personal integrity of those who asserted it (Carrington, 1984).

As originally formulated, the indeterminacy thesis was never merely a theoretical exercise. It was also politically motivated. In particular, it aimed to subvert two important mainstream theories of law: *formalism*, which holds that the application of legal language to a particular case always, or almost always, is capable of producing one and only one legally correct answer; and *functionalism*, which holds that legal rules and practices tend to produce consistent results that are "needed" or "wanted" by society. In its simplest and most radical form, the indeterminacy thesis claims that there is no such thing as an easy case in the law, that the choice of result in any given case is contingent on countless extralegal factors, and that the legal system as a whole is therefore an inherently political enterprise no matter what judges and lawyers may think and say about it.

98   *Difference between ambiguity and treachery*

In general, the CLS claim was not (or not only) that the legal system is political in the narrow sense of a stealthy extension to the judicial sphere of policy struggles between political parties – as if Democratic judges consciously sought to advance the policies espoused by their party, while Republican judges consciously sought to advance the policies espoused by theirs. Although this sort of thing does happen sometimes[2] – and may even be happening more and more often since the Trump era began – the word "political" in the CLS critique of legal determinacy actually had a much broader meaning. The indeterminacy thesis holds that even quintessentially good-faith "legal" results in courtrooms depend on judicial value-choices that are not themselves dictated by antecedent legal authority. They are caused by *something else*, whether or not a given judge is aware of it. What the judge had or did not have for breakfast, for example – and I mean this quite literally (see Danziger, Levav, & Avnaim-Pesso, 2011). Or, more broadly, the way that the judge's own social position and upbringing affect his or her sense of interpretive possibilities. On this view, law chugs along as "law," and not as politics, because the people who tend to do law and consume legal writing are not aware of their own ideological biases.

The law-is-politics argument undoubtedly sounded far more dangerous to the average mainstream legal academic in the 1990s than it does today. The legal indeterminacy claim questioned the truth of the anodyne conventional distinction between small-d democratic conflicts over values in the legislature and legal disputes in courtrooms, which are supposed to be settled by the neutral, nonpartisan application of legal rules and principles. Not only that, the indeterminacy thesis seemed to subvert faith in the rule of law itself, which is why one particularly strident critic of CLS had controversially called on its proponents "to depart the law school, perhaps to seek a place elsewhere in the academy" (Carrington, 1984: 227).

Because so much of legal practice and legal education is rhetorical, in the classical sense of an exercise in the art of persuasion, law professors tend to be wary of admitting things up front. Perhaps my colleague worried that if he admitted that Magritte's painting is only one image of one type of pipe, and not "a pipe," then I would somehow try to brow-beat him into agreeing with the CLS critique of legal determinacy, and, even more gallingly, with the mysterious, and no doubt to him dangerous, practice of. . . [wait for ominous-sounding music] . . . *deconstruction*.

Deconstruction

Only a couple of years prior to the Magritte conversation leading critical legal scholars in the UK had begun to appropriate the notion of deconstruction from the writings of the French philosopher and social theorist Jacques Derrida

Difference between ambiguity and treachery 99

(Douzinas, Warrington, & McVeigh, 1991). Derrida's inspiration for choosing the word "deconstruction" was Martin Heidegger's use of the term *Destruktion* ("destruction"). Heidegger's insight that we are all historical (*geschichtlich*) beings who do not stand *in* history, but rather are always already constantly *making* it in the here-and-now, radically reinterpreted the concept of the human being. No longer a self-enclosed Aristotelian rational animal or Cartesian thinking-subject-amongst-objects, Heidegger's human being ceased being a noun and became a gerund: a "being-there" (*Dasein*). After Heidegger, it became theoretically impossible to think and speak definitively about anything at all – least of all human nature – without first acknowledging – and worrying – that one's thoughts and words always are, first and foremost, crudely contingent historical artifacts rather than ahistorical, objective truths.

Loosely speaking, Derrida's "deconstruction" married Heidegger's philosophy with what Richard Rorty had called the twentieth century's "linguistic turn" (1967): the greatly increased focus by serious analytic and continental philosophers on the relationship between philosophy and language (Caputo, 1997: 32). Now, it is true that even a minimally competent discussion of Derrida's own uses of the term "deconstruction" would have to be extremely subtle and complex, to say the least. But it is not necessary to do that here, since we happen to be talking about the sizzle of deconstruction, not the steak. For at the time of our brief conversation about "The Treachery of Images," sizzle aplenty was probably all that my colleague had heard or seen reported about academic renegades like me who took deconstruction seriously enough to believe that it might be relevant to legal theory.

At their most basic level, all sophisticated versions of the indeterminacy thesis are about the logical – *not* the practical – ambiguity of language and images. History, including the history that we are always already making here-and-now, contains paths both taken and untaken. This implies that at any given moment in time there are always linguistic resources available that would allow us to go in many different directions from a given starting point. If, in any given case, a rule of law or justice says "X," and historically plausible arguments can be made that this rule as applied supports two inconsistent results, then it follows that "X" is logically ambiguous. The fact that much or most of the time "X" actually *is* received by similarly situated legal actors as unambiguous is no rebuttal, for as Pindar's ancient poem on *nomos* (custom) says, that sort of phenomenon is explained by customary ways of receiving language, not by disembodied logic.

Deconstruction takes satisfaction in demonstrating these kinds of ambiguities in case after case after case. Here is the alarming way that one commentator described, "in a nutshell" (and thus reductively), what deconstruction is all about: "Whenever deconstruction finds a nutshell – a secure axiom or a pithy maxim – the very idea is to crack it open and disturb this tranquility"

100 *Difference between ambiguity and treachery*

(Caputo, 1997: 32). It is true that Derrida himself adamantly refused to reduce the notion of deconstruction to the status of a mere technique for demonstrating ambiguity. For him, deconstruction was something that is always already happening in our world whether or not we are trying to "do" it (see Derrida, 1990). Nevertheless, to demonstrate ambiguity in any given case – even a case that most lawyers would call "easy" – is what critical legal scholars at the time would have called an exercise in deconstruction.

I got the distinct impression at the time that my colleague was treating my use of Magritte's picture as an attempt to make a similarly maddening deconstructive point about the image painted there. I could be wrong, but my colleague might have seen this picture as an "easy case" that could not reasonably, under any circumstances, *not* be interpreted as the image of a pipe.

What a terrible affront to law and legal education the anarchic-seeming practice of deconstruction must have created in the minds of people, like my colleague, for whom the integrity and stability of the law was seen as the *sine qua non* of any just society governed by the rule of law! There are few endeavors more committed than the law is to the principle that language is capable of objectively determining its meaning and application. After all, people's lives and fortunes can rise or fall on the basis of the supposedly neutral and objective application of legal rules. To have them rise and fall on the basis of history and custom alone looks . . . a lot less just. Much seems to depend on "taking rights seriously," as the liberal legal philosopher Ronald Dworkin put it in his 1978 book by that name, and this seems to imply that much depends on people believing in the absolute metaphysical security of there being "right answers" to all or most legal questions where people's rights are at stake.

If the clearest possible picture of a pipe could be seen, with equal validity, to depict a soup ladle, a hammer, a horse, or even nothing at all, then by further extension of the deconstructive argument my colleague might have been forced to admit that, legally speaking, even the plainest act of murder is also plausibly not a murder, even the clearest act of negligence is also plausibly not an act of negligence, and so on and so on, until the coat of many colors that is the law comes apart at the seams. I imagine he feared that I was laying a trap – that if he conceded the point that Magritte's unambiguously painted pipe is not a pipe, then I would shout "Gotcha!" and compel him to substitute the then-ubiquitous CLS slogan, "Law is politics," for whatever conventional idea of the rule of law he happened to believe in.

The treachery of ambiguity versus the ambiguity of treachery

Of course, his suspicion that my intention was to destabilize his faith in the rule of law would have been correct if, instead of "The Treachery of Images," I had chosen to show him a picture of, say, the kind of drawing that

Difference between ambiguity and treachery 101

Figure 5.2 A duck-rabbit

psychologist Joseph Jastrow and philosopher Ludwig Wittgenstein called a "duck-rabbit."[3]

Figure 5.2 is unquestionably a single representation: materially speaking it is but one picture, not two. But it *can* be seen in at least two different "aspects." Looking at it one way, it depicts a duck whose head is turned to the left. Looking at it a different way, it depicts a rabbit whose head is turned to the right. Interestingly enough, it appears that human perception is such that these two different aspects can be seen continuously as a duck *or* a rabbit, but not as both at the same time. (Try it yourself and you'll see what I mean.)

More importantly, it is possible that someone does not notice the ambiguity of the image, in which case they would perceive it solely as a duck, or solely as a rabbit. Wittgenstein called this sort of person "aspect-blind" (1953: 213e). The British legal philosopher H. L. A. Hart, certainly no naïf when it came to appreciating law's many ambiguities, inadvertently expressed the creed of a legally intelligent aspect-blind person when he claimed that legal rules "must [have] a core of settled meaning," even if "there will be, as well, a penumbra of debatable cases in which words are neither obviously applicable nor obviously ruled out" (1958: 607).

Unrecognized ambiguities can prove hazardous to those who fail to recognize them. In particular, the creative revelation of ambiguity in what appears to be an absolutely clear case must seem inherently treacherous to an aspect-blind person. The oldest (and perhaps clearest) example of this kind of phenomenon is the tale told in Book 9 of the *Odyssey*.

102 *Difference between ambiguity and treachery*

The tale of Odysseus and Polyphemus

Odysseus and his men found themselves trapped on Sicily and held captive inside the cave of Polyphemus, a giant cyclops fathered by the god Poseidon with the sea-nymph Thoösa. After Polyphemus ate two of his compatriots, Odysseus offered him some strong wine that his crew had acquired earlier in their journey. Polyphemus proceeded to get drunk and fall asleep. Clever Odysseus then stabbed him in his single eye with a hardened wooden stake, blinding him.

Before falling asleep, however, Polyphemus had asked Odysseus for his name, whereupon the latter lied by saying that his name was *outis*, which means "nobody" in Greek (*nemo*, in Latin). Startled awake by Odysseus's attack, Polyphemus staggered blindly out of the cave in a rage, calling for help to his brother cyclopes who lived on the island. The others heard his cries and came. But after Polyphemus told them that *outis* (nobody) had hurt him, the other cyclopes concluded that it was the gods, not men, who had afflicted him with blindness. They recommended that he pray to the gods for help, and then they turned away from the cave and went home, allowing Odysseus and his men to escape.

In Greek, the name *outis* and the pronoun *outis* are homonyms and homographs. Saying *outis* out loud to Polyphemus, as Odysseus did, knowing or hoping that this word would be misinterpreted and relied upon: *that* is just about as clear an example of ambiguity used treacherously as you can get.

At least on the face of it, this sort of treachery seems unethical. Indeed, some philosophers, Kant for example, have even gone so far as to say that the moral duty to be honest and truthful to others is unconditional, even if the Other is a bloodthirsty would-be murderer (Kant, 1996: 611–15). Although I must confess to harboring some doubt about whether old man Kant would have done any differently had he found himself spirited out of Königsberg and tumbled into Polyphemus's cave.

But of course the treachery of ambiguity is not the only kind of treachery there is. To understand the critical importance of this point, it is useful to compare the foregoing story of Odysseus and Polyphemus with the even better-known tale of the Trojan Horse. The account of the latter incident is traditionally patched together from two sources: a couple of lines in the *Odyssey,* and the more elaborate treatment of the story found in Book 2 of Virgil's *Aeneid.*

The tale of the Trojan Horse

After waging ten years of brutal war during their siege of Troy, the Greeks seemed to give up. They sailed away over the horizon, leaving

Difference between ambiguity and treachery 103

behind a huge sculpture of a horse as an offering to the goddess Athena, seemingly in atonement for their desecration of her temple there. The Trojans, believing that the war was at long last over, were so delighted by the gift that, ignoring the advice of their high priest Laocoön, they proceeded to tow the sculpture inside the city walls. We all remember what happened next: the city fell and the Trojans were massacred when, after nightfall, Odysseus and his fellow Greek sappers crawled out of the belly of the horse and opened the city's gates to let in Agamemnon's army, which by that time had secretly sailed back to Troy. But observe carefully: the Trojan Horse was not a problem for the Trojans because it was possibly the sculpture of a pig or a goat, and therefore an ambiguous *object*. It was a problem because the Trojans thought that it was actually was meant to be a gift to the goddess rather than what it was really meant to be: a troop transport.

Like the story of the Trojan Horse, the most important lesson to be drawn from Magritte's painting of a pipe is that an image – any image – is always tempting us to confuse it with reality. Unlike the figure of the duck-rabbit, Magritte's painting of a pipe is not really about the *ambiguity* of images. It is not even about the treachery of an ambiguous image. Assume for the moment that a pipe is just unambiguously a pipe, and that Magritte's picture of a pipe is just unambiguously a picture of a pipe. By far the most interesting philosophical aspect of Magritte's painting is not that it could be interpreted to be a picture of something else, but rather that we are tempted to accept it as an absolute mirror of reality itself. As its title suggests, the painting is about the *treachery* of images that present themselves to us *as* unambiguous. And let's be blunt about it: everyone on earth is more-or-less constantly perceiving things and situations as unambiguous in daily life. Images are treacherous in this primordial way *long before* they can be consciously interpreted as ambiguous or unambiguous.

One of Wittgenstein's greatest insights was to realize that the experience of looking at images (such as "The Treachery of Images" and the duck-rabbit) is similar to the experience of looking at written language in one important respect: both familiar pictures and familiar words seem to "look" at us in a meaningful way. These words come to acquire a "familiar physiognomy" for us, a curious phenomenon that Wittgenstein describes as "the feeling that [a word] has taken up its meaning into itself, that it is an actual likeness of its meaning" (1953: 218e).

But of course, neither images nor words actually have real eyeballs to look at us with. Nor do they have little hands that could bear their messages to us over the distance, however small, that stands between us and them. In truth, they just display . . . only themselves. It is *we* who look at and understand them; *we* who grasp what *we* take to be their messages.

The ethics of self-treachery

During the waning days of the CLS movement in America, critics of the indeterminacy thesis believed they had found what Richard Fischl ironically called "the question that killed critical legal studies" (1992). That question asked the prophets of indeterminacy to describe what arrangements they would put in place of the liberal legal order, built as it is on faith in the rule of law and therefore an outright rejection, at least in public, of the indeterminacy thesis.

When answers to that question either were not forthcoming or were felt to be too sketchy and unrealistic to be believed, liberal critics of the indeterminacy thesis tended to write things like this: "It is impossible not to harbor skepticism about an intellectual movement that asks us to adhere to it on the basis of faith alone and to pledge that faith for wholly unknown or unrevealed objectives" (Massey, 1992: 829). The critics of CLS thought that the indeterminacy thesis and the deconstruction that demonstrated it were irresponsibly anarchic political maneuvers. Until the publication in 1992 of Simon Critchley's seminal book, *The Ethics of Deconstruction* (2014) – and even after – they failed to recognize or acknowledge that deconstructive discourse is mainly intended to emphasize the personal moral responsibility of those who enforce the law – most especially the moral responsibility of those legal actors who harbor the ethically dangerous illusion that the words of the law, together with well-settled legal practices, are themselves doing all the work.

Aristotle thought that the present existence of concrete beings were composed of two elements: their inherent possibilities for being this or that – in Greek, their *dynamis* (*potentia*, in Latin) – and the particular way in which they actualized their possibilities at any given point in time (their *energeia*, or *actus*, in Latin). Legal words are infinitely interpretable only if we think of them as presently "containing" all their possible interpretations in the same way that Aristotle thought that material objects presently contain all of their possibilities for being. But that's not the way it is. Our own everyday experiences with words should prove to us that the *potential* ambiguity of legal texts is not the same as their *actual* ambiguity, considered as a real, lived phenomenon.

"The naïve men are easy to fool," said the pre-Socratic philosopher Bias of Priene. It is possible – likely even – that political action, to be effective, needs useful idiots (or at least useful innocents) who know not what they have done. First and foremost, however, the treachery of the words that we use, or allow to be used, to deceive *ourselves* in order to inflict legalized suffering on others in good conscience poses an ethical problem no less than a political one. The decision to bear this sort of treachery in mind *avant l'acte* is itself an ethical deed: it manifests the Self's forthright acceptance of what we have called its *pre*sponsibility to and for the Other. Anticipating a personal sense of *re*sponsibility based on the Self's radical freedom *avant la lettre*, this decision can only lead to what Adam Gearey has rightly called an "ethics of anxiety" (2018: 21).

"Ah Bartleby! Ah humanity!" (Melville, 1984: 607). I wish my colleague were alive today (he's not) so that I could get off the high horse he thought I was on and tell him that I, too, am a naïve fool when it comes to thinking about law and justice, as is everyone else I know. The main purpose of this book has been to identify and expose the poignancy and the ethical implications of this last, most important insight.

Notes

1 1929. Oil on canvas, by René Magritte (1898–1967) © C. Herscovici/Artists Rights Society (ARS), New York.
2 See, e.g., Bush v. Gore, 531 U.S. 98 (2000), concerning which one commentator asserted at the time: "[T]he decision in the Florida election case may be ranked as the single most corrupt decision in Supreme Court history, because it is the only one that I know of where the majority justices decided as they did because of the personal identity and political affiliation of the litigants. This was cheating, and a violation of the judicial oath" (Dershowitz, 2001: 174).
3 The image shown here first appeared as an unattributed drawing in the October 23, 1892, issue of *Fliegende Blätter*, a German humor magazine. Jastrow then adopted it to illustrate the ambiguity of perception in *Fact and Fable in Psychology* (1900: 278).Wittgenstein states that he derived his own figure of the duck-rabbit from Jastrow's book (1953: 194e).

References

ABA (American Bar Association) 2018, "Model Code of Judicial Conduct." Available at: www.americanbar.org/groups/professional_responsibility/-publications/model_code_of_judicial_conduct/

Abelson, R. & Nielsen, K. 1967, "History of Ethics," in P. Edwards (ed.), *The Encyclopedia of Philosophy*, Macmillan, New York, vol. 3, pp. 81–117.

Adorno, T. 2005, *Minima Moralia: Reflections From a Damaged Life*, trans. E. F. N. Jephcott, Verso, London.

Adorno, T. 1973, *Negative Dialectics*, trans. E. B. Ashton, Routledge, London.

Adorno, T. & Benjamin, W. 1999, *The Complete Correspondence 1928–1940*, ed. H. Lonitz, trans. N. Walker, Harvard University Press, Cambridge, MA.

Aeschylus, 1906, "Eumenides," in id, *Plays*, trans. G. M. Cookson, J. M. Dent & Sons, London, pp. 299–339.

Alexander, M. 2012, *The New Jim Crow: Mass Incarceration in the Age of Colorblindness*, The New Press, New York.

Aquinas, T. 1940, "The Summa Theologica," in Anton Pegis (ed.), *Introduction to St. Thomas Aquinas*, Modern Library, New York, passim.

Arendt, H. 1958, *The Human Condition*, University of Chicago Press, Chicago.

Aristotle 1934, *Nicomachean Ethics*, trans. H. Rackham, Harvard University Press, Cambridge, MA.

Austin, J. 1998, *The Province of Jurisprudence Determined*, eds. D. Campbell & P. Thomas, Ashgate, Aldershot.

Balkin, J. 2020, "AMA: Chris Green Asks About the Oath," June 22. Available at: https://balkin.blogspot.com/2020/06/ama-chris-green-asks-about-oath.html

Balkin, J. 1998, *Cultural Software: A Theory of Ideology*, Yale University Press, New Haven, CT.

Baltzly, D. 2018, "Stoicism," *Stanford Encyclopedia of Philosophy*. Available at: https://plato.stanford.edu/entries/stoicism/#Eth

Benjamin, W. 1999, *The Arcades Project*, trans. H. Weiland & K. McLaughlin, Harvard University Press, Cambridge, MA.

Benjamin, W. 1978, *Reflections: Essays, Aphorisms, Autobiographical Writings*, trans. E. Jephcott, Schocken Books, New York.

Benjamin, W. 1968, *Illuminations: Essays and Reflections*, trans. H. Zohn, Schocken Books, New York.

Bentham, J. 1970, *Of Laws in General*, ed. H. L. A. Hart, Athlone Press, London.

References 107

Bentham, J. 1939, "An Introduction to the Principles of Morals and Legislation," in E. Burtt (ed.), *The English Philosophers From Bacon to Mill*, Modern Library, New York.

Berger, P. & Luckmann, T. 1967, *The Social Construction of Reality*, Doubleday, New York.

Boethius 2012, *The Consolation of Philosophy*, Ignatius Press, San Francisco.

Bonhoeffer, D. 1977, *Letters and Papers From Prison*, ed. E. Bethge, Simon & Schuster, New York.

Borrajo, M. 1968, "Situation Ethics in the Light of Vatican II," *Dominicana Journal*, vol. 53(3), pp. 231–41. Available at: www.dominicanajournal.org/wp-content/files/old-journal-archive/vol53/no3/dominicanav53n3situationethicslightvaticanii.pdf

Bouwsma, O. K. 1986, *Ludwig Wittgenstein: Conversations 1949–1951*, eds. J. L. Craft & R. Hustwit, Hackett, Indianapolis.

Bradwell v. Illinois, 83 U.S. 130, 141 (1872) (concurring opinion).

Brown, W. 1999, *The Ethos of the Cosmos: The Genesis of Moral Imagination in the Bible*, William B. Eerdmans, Grand Rapids, MI.

Buber, M. 2000, *I and Thou*, trans. R. Smith, Scribner, New York.

Burgo, B. 2011, "Emmanuel Levinas," *Stanford Encyclopedia of Philosophy*. Available at: https://plato.stanford.edu/entries/levinas/

Camus, A. 1965, *Notebooks 1942–1951*, trans. J. O'Brien, Alfred A. Knopf, New York.

Cantú, F. 2019, "Has Any One of Us Wept?" *New York Review of Books* (January 17), pp. 4–6.

Caputo, J. 1997, *Deconstruction in a Nutshell: A Conversation With Jacques Derrida*, Fordham University Press, New York.

Carrington, P. 1984, "Of Law and the River," *Journal of Legal Education*, vol. 34, pp. 222–28.

Carson, A. 1999, *Economy of the Unlost*, Princeton University Press, Princeton, NJ.

Chekhov, A. 2003 [1892], *Ward No. 6 and Other Stories*, trans. C. Garnett, Barnes & Noble Classics, New York.

Cohon, R. 2018, "Hume's Moral Philosophy," *Stanford Encyclopedia of Philosophy*. Available at: https://plato.stanford.edu/entries/hume-moral/#ear

Cover, R. 1984, *Justice Accused: Antislavery and the Judicial Process*, Yale University Press, New Haven, CT.

Critchley, S. 2014, *The Ethics of Deconstruction: Derrida and Levinas*, 3rd ed., Edinburgh University Press, Edinburgh.

Danziger, S., Levav, J. & Avnaim-Pesso, L. 2011, "Extraneous Factors in Judicial Decisions," *Proceedings of the National Academy of Sciences (PNAS)*. Available at: www.pnas.org/content/108/17/6889

Delgado, R. (ed.) 1995, *Critical Race Theory: The Cutting Edge*, Temple University Press, Philadelphia.

Derrida, J. 1990, "Force of Law: The 'Mystical Foundation of Authority,'" trans. M. Quaintance, *Cardozo Law Review*, vol. 11, pp. 919–1045.

Derrida, J., Gadamer, H. G. & Lacoue-Labarthe, P. 2016, *Heidegger, Philosophy, and Politics: The Heidelberg Conference*, ed. M. Calle-Gruber, trans. J. Fort, Fordham University Press, New York.

Dershowitz, A. 2001, *Supreme Injustice: How the High Court Hijacked Election 2000*, Oxford University Press, Oxford.

108 References

Descartes, R. 1984, *The Philosophical Writings of Descartes*, 2 vols., trans. J. Cottingham, R. Stoothoff & D. Murdoch, Cambridge University Press, Cambridge.

Diogenes Laërtius 2018, *Lives of the Eminent Philosophers*, ed. J. Miller, trans. P. Mensch, Oxford University Press, Oxford.

Douzinas, C., Warrington, R. & McVeigh, S. 1991, *Postmodern Jurisprudence: The Law of Text in the Texts of Law*, Routledge, London.

Dworkin, R. 1986, *Law's Empire*, Harvard University Press, Cambridge, MA.

Dworkin, R. 1977, *Taking Rights Seriously*, Harvard University Press, Cambridge, MA.

Ewing, A. C. 1948, *The Definition of Good*, Routledge & Kegan Paul, London.

Featherstone, M. 1993, "Global and Local Cultures," in J. Bird et al. (eds.), *Mapping the Futures: Local Cultures, Global Change*, Routledge, London, pp. 169–87.

Finnis, J. 1984, "The Authority of Law in the Predicament of Contemporary Social Theory," *Notre Dame Journal of Law, Ethics & Public Policy*, vol. 1(1), pp. 115–37.

Fischl, R. 1992, "The Question That Killed Critical Legal Studies," *Law & Social Inquiry*, vol. 17, pp. 779–820.

Fisher, W., Horwitz, M. & Reed, T. (eds.) 1993, *American Legal Realism*, Oxford University Press, Oxford.

Foucault, M. 1980, *Power/Knowledge: Selected Interviews and Other Writings 1972–1977*, ed. C. Gordon, trans. C. Gordon et al., Pantheon, New York.

Fukuyama, F. 2006 [1992], *The End of History and the Last Man*, rev. ed., The Free Press, New York.

Fuller, L. 1969, *The Morality of Law*, rev. ed., Yale University Press, New Haven, CT.

Fuller, L. 1958, "Positivism and Fidelity to Law – A Reply to Professor Hart," *Harvard Law Review*, vol. 71(4), pp. 630–72.

Fuller, L. 1948, "What Law Schools Can Contribute to the Making of Lawyers," *Journal of Legal Education*, vol. 1, pp. 189–204.

Gallagher, E. 2018, "History on Trial: The Literature of Justification," *Lehigh University Digital Library*. Available at: http://digital.lib.lehigh.edu/trial/justification/

Gearey, A. 2018, *Poverty Law and Legal Activism: Lives That Slide Out of View*, Routledge, Milton Park, Abingdon, Oxon.

Goethe, J. W. 1971 [1809], *Elective Affinities*, trans. R. J. Hollingdale, Penguin Books, London.

Goethe, J. W. 1964, *Goethe: Selected Verse*, ed. & trans. D. Luke, Penguin Books, London.

Gramsci, A. 1971, *Selections From the Prison Notebooks*, trans. Q. Hoare & G. Smith, International Publishers, New York.

Grannan, C. 2020, "What's the Difference Between Morality and Ethics?" *Encyclopaedia Britannica*. Available at: www.britannica.com/story/whats-the-difference-between-morality-and-ethics

Grossman, V. 1985, *Life and Fate*, trans. R. Chandler, Harper & Row, New York.

Halliday, M. A. K. & Hasan, R. 1976, *Cohesion in English*, Longman, London.

Hampton, J. 1984, "The Moral Education Theory of Punishment," *Philosophy & Public Affairs*, vol. 13(3), pp. 208–38.

Hart, H. L. A. 1961, *The Concept of Law*, Oxford University Press, Oxford.

References 109

Hart, H. L. A. 1958, "Positivism and the Separation of Law and Morals," *Harvard Law Review*, vol. 71, pp. 593–629.

Haynes, E. 1944, *The Selection and Tenure of Judges*, National Conference of Judicial Councils, Newark, NJ.

Hegel, G. W. F. 1977, *Phenomenology of Spirit*, trans. A. V. Miller, Oxford University Press, Oxford.

Hegel, G. W. F. 1967, *Philosophy of Right*, trans. T. M. Knox, Oxford University Press, Oxford.

Heidegger, M. 1984, *The Metaphysical Foundations of Logic*, trans. M. Heim, Indiana University Press, Bloomington.

Heidegger, M. 1962, *Being and Time*, trans. J. Macquarrie & E. Robinson, HarperCollins, New York.

Heidegger, M. & Fink, E. 1993, *Heraclitus Seminar*, trans. C. Sebert, Northwestern University Press, Evanston, IL.

Heinze, E. 2013, *The Concept of Injustice*, Routledge, Milton Park, Abingdon, Oxon.

Heraclitus 1987, *Fragments*, trans. T. M. Robinson, University of Toronto Press, Toronto.

Hesiod 1996, "Theogony," in K. Atchity (ed.), *The Classical Greek Reader*, Henry Holt, New York, pp. 20–27.

Hickley, C. 2020, "National Gallery of Art Returns a Picasso Work to Settle Claim: The Heirs of a Jewish Banker Said the Portrait of a Woman Was Among the Works He Sold Under Duress When the Nazis Took Power," *New York Times*, April 2. Available at: www.nytimes.com/2020/03/31/arts/design/picasso-national-gallery-of-art-heirs.html

Higginbottom, K. 2017, "The Price of Being a Whistleblower," *Forbes*, February 18. Available at: www.forbes.com/sites/karenhigginbottom/2017/02/18/the-price-of-being-a-whistleblower/#d47635f5b525/

Hobbes, T. 1914 [1651], *Leviathan*, J. M. Dent, London.

Hochschild, A. 2019, "Family Values," *New York Review of Books* (September), pp. 72–73.

Holmes, O. W. 1963, *The Common Law*, ed. M. deW. Howe, Little, Brown, sBoston, MA.

HR (United States House of Representatives) 2011, "Code of Official Conduct." Available at: https://ethics.house.gov/publications/code-official-conduct

Hume, D. 1985 [1738], *A Treatise of Human Nature*, Penguin Books, New York.

Husserl, E. 1990, *On the Phenomenology of the Consciousness of Internal Time (1893–1917)*, trans. J. B. Brough, Kluwer Academic Publishers, Dordrecht.

Husserl, E. 1970, *The Crisis of European Sciences and Transcendental Phenomenology*, trans. D. Carr, Northwestern University Press, Evanston, IL.

Hyppolite, J. 1996, *Introduction to Hegel's Philosophy of History*, trans. B. Harris & J. Spurlock, University of Florida Press, Gainesville.

Ihrig, S. 2016, *Justifying Genocide: Germany and the Armenians From Bismarck to Hitler*, Harvard University Press, Cambridge, MA.

IIT (Illinois Institute of Technology) 2011, *Code of Ethics for Public Officers and Employees*. Available at: http://ethics.iit.edu/ecodes/node/5282

110   *References*

IIT (Illinois Institute of Technology) 1991, *Law Enforcement Code of Conduct*. Available at: http://ethics.iit.edu/ecodes/node/4624

Jastrow, J. 1900, *Fact and Fable in Psychology*, Houghton Mifflin, New York.

Jefferson, T. 1999, *Notes on the State of Virginia*, Penguin Books, New York.

Jones, J. 1993, *Bad Blood: The Tuskegee Syphilis Experiment*, rev. ed., The Free Press, New York.

Juvenal 2004, "Satires," No. VI, lines 347–48, in *Juvenal and Persius*, trans. S. M. Brand, Loeb Classical Library, Cambridge, MA.

Kafka, F. 1983, "Before the Law," in id, *The Complete Stories*, ed. Nahum Glatzer, trans. W. & E. Muir, Schocken Books, New York, pp. 3–4.

Kairys, D. (ed.) 1990, *The Politics of Law: A Progressive Critique*, rev. ed., Pantheon Books, New York.

Kant, I. 2014 [1786], "What Does It Mean to Orient Oneself in Thinking?" (1786), trans. D. Ferrer. Available at: https://ia800300.us.archive.org/4/items/KantOrient FerrerMarch2014/KantOrientFerrerMarch2014.pdf

Kant, I. 1998, *The Critique of Pure Reason*, trans. P. Guyer & A. Wood, Cambridge University Press, Cambridge.

Kant, I. 1996, *Practical Philosophy*, trans. M. Gregor, Cambridge University Press, Cambridge.

Kennedy, D. 1976, "Form and Substance in Private Law Adjudication," *Harvard Law Review*, vol. 89, pp. 1685–778.

Kelman, M. 1987, *A Guide to Critical Legal Studies*, Harvard University Press, Cambridge.

Kierkegaard, S. 1993, *The Diary of Søren Kierkegaard*, ed. P. Rohde, Citadel Press, New York.

Lacey, A. R. 1986, *A Dictionary of Philosophy*, 2nd ed., Routledge, London.

Leibniz, G. 2017, *Theodicy: Essays on the Goodness of God, the Freedom of Man and the Origin of Evil*, Pinnacle Books, Canton, OH.

Leibniz, G. 1934, "The Monadology," in *Leibniz: Philosophical Writings*, trans. M. Morris, J. M. Dent, London, pp. 3–20.

Levin, I. 1972, *The Stepford Wives*, Random House, New York.

Levinas, E. 2001, *Is It Righteous to Be? Interviews With Emmanuel Levinas*, ed. J. Robbins, Stanford University Press, Stanford.

Levinas, E. 1999, *Alterity and Transcendence*, trans. M. Smith, Columbia University Press, New York.

Levinas, E. 1998, *On Thinking-of-the-Other Entre Nous*, trans. M. Smith & B. Harshav, Columbia University Press, New York.

Levinas, E. 1996, *Basic Philosophical Writings*, eds. A. Peperzak et al., Indiana University Press, Bloomington.

Lincoln, A. 1865, "Lincoln's Second Inaugural," March 4. Available at: www.nps. gov/linc/learn/historyculture/lincoln-second-inaugural.htm

Locke, J. 1939a, "An Essay Concerning Human Understanding," in E. Burtt (ed.), *The English Philosophers From Bacon to Mill*, Modern Library, New York, pp. 235–402.

Locke, J. 1939b, "An Essay Concerning the True and Original Extent of Civil Government," in E. Burtt (ed.), *The English Philosophers From Bacon to Mill*, Modern Library, New York, pp. 403–503.

References 111

Löwy, M. 2004, "The Concept of Elective Affinity According to Max Weber," *Archives de sciences sociales des religions*, vol. 127, p. 6. Available at: www.cairn. info/journal-archives-de-sciences-sociales-des-religions-2004-3-page-6.htm

Maimonides, M. 2011, *Guide for the Perplexed*, Empire Books, New York.

Mannheim, K. 1985 [1936], *Ideology and Utopia: An Introduction to the Sociology of Knowledge*, trans. L. Wirth & E. Shils, Harcourt Brace Jovanovich, San Diego, CA.

Marx, K. 1959, *Basic Writings on Politics and Philosophy*, Anchor Books, Garden City, NY.

Massey, C. 1992, "The Faith Healers," *Law & Social Inquiry*, vol. 17, pp. 821–29.

McCarthy-Jones, S. 2018, "Survivors of Sexual Violence Are Let Down by the Criminal Justice System – Here's What Should Happen Next," *The Conversation*, March 29. Available at: https://theconversation.com/survivors-of-sexual-vio-lence-are-let-down-by-the-criminal-justice-system-heres-what-should-happen-next-94138

McGuinness, B. (ed.) 1979, *Wittgenstein and the Vienna Circle: Conversations Recorded by Friedrich Waismann*, trans. J. Schulte & B. McGuinness, Basil Blackwell, Oxford.

Meeropol, R. 2003, *An Execution in the Family: One Son's Journey*, St. Martin's Press, New York.

Melville, H. 1984 [1856], "Bartleby," in *Herman Melville: Masters Library Edition*, Octopus Books, New York, pp. 583-607.

Mill, J. S. 1939, "Utilitarianism," in E. Burtt (ed.), *The English Philosophers From Bacon to Mill*, Modern Library, New York, pp. 895–948.

Milosz, C. 1990, *The Captive Mind*, trans. J. Zielonko, Vintage Books, New York.

Morris, D. 2016, "Accommodating Nazi Tyranny? The Wrong Turn of the Social Democratic Legal Philosopher Gustav Radbruch," *Law & History Review*, vol. 34, pp. 649–88.

Mount, F. 2019, "Nasty, Brutish, and Great," *New York Review of Books* (June 6), pp. 22–24.

Muller, R. 2016, "Death Penalty May Not Bring Peace to Victims' Families," *Psychology Today*, October 19. Available at: www.psychologytoday.com/us/blog/talking-about-trauma/201610/death-penalty-may-not-bring-peace-victims-families

Nietzsche, F. 1968, *The Will to Power*, ed. W. Kaufmann, trans. W. Kaufmann & R. J. Hollingdale, Vintage Books, New York.

Nietzsche, F. 1961, *Thus Spoke Zarathustra: A Book for Everyone and No One*, trans. R. J. Hollingdale, Penguin Classics, New York.

Nietzsche, F. 1954, "Beyond Good and Evil," in *The Philosophy of Nietzsche*, trans. Horace Samuel, Modern Library, New York, pp. 369-616.

Nozick, R. 1974, *Anarchy, State, and Utopia*, Basic Books, New York.

Oppen, G. 2007, *Selected Prose, Daybooks, and Papers*, ed. S. Cope, University of California Press, Berkeley.

Orwell, G. 1995, *Animal Farm: A Fairy Story*, Harcourt Brace, New York.

Parmenides of Elea 1984, *Fragments*, trans. D. Gallop, University of Toronto Press, Toronto.

Pascal, B. 1941, *Pensées and the Provincial Letters*, trans. W. F. Trotter & T. M'Crie, Modern Library, New York.

112   *References*

Patrick, G. 1913, "The New Optimism," *Popular Science Monthly*, vol. 82, pp. 492–503. Available at: https://en.wikisource.org/wiki/Popular_Science_Monthly/Volume_82/May_1913/The_New_Optimism

Paulson, S. 2006, "On the Background and Significance of Gustav Radbruch's Post-War Papers," *Oxford Journal of Legal Studies*, vol. 26, pp. 17–40.

Pindar 1938, "The Power of Custom," in T. F. Higham & C. M. Bowra (eds.), *The Oxford Book of Greek Verse in Translation*, trans. C. M. Bowra, Oxford University Press, Oxford, p. 296.

Pirsig, M., Glendon, M. & Alford, W. 2020, "Legal Ethics," *Encyclopaedia Britannica*. Available at: www.britannica.com/topic/legal-ethics

Plutarch 1950, "Solon," in id, *Twelve Lives*, trans. J. Dryden, Fine Editions Press, Cleveland, OH, pp. 81–107.

Popper, K. 1963, *Conjectures and Refutations: The Growth of Scientific Knowledge*, Routledge, London.

Rae, N. 2018, *The Great Stain: Witnessing American Slavery*, Harry N. Abrams, New York.

Rawls, J. 1971, *A Theory of Justice*, Harvard University Press, Cambridge, MA.

Raz, J. 1999, "The Obligation to Obey: Revision and Tradition," in William Edmonson (ed.), *The Duty to Obey the Law: Selected Philosophical Readings*, Rowman & Littlefield, Oxford, pp. 159–75.

Rhode, D. 2006, "The Professional Ethics of Professors," *Journal of Legal Education*, vol. 56, pp. 70–85.

Rorty, R. (ed.) 1967, *The Linguistic Turn: Essays in Philosophical Method*, University of Chicago Press, Chicago.

Rousseau, J. 1993a [1755], "A Discourse on the Origin of Inequality," in *The Social Contract and the Discourses*, trans. G. D. H. Cole, Everyman's Library, New York, pp. 31–125.

Rousseau, J. 1993b [1762], "The Social Contract," in *The Social Contract and the Discourses*, trans. G. D. H. Cole, Everyman's Library, New York, pp. 179–305.

Rrenban, M. 2004, *Wild, Unforgettable Philosophy in the Early Works of Walter Benjamin*, Lexington Books, Washington, DC.

Sartre, J. P. 1989, "No Exit," in id, *No Exit and Three Other Plays*, trans. S. Gilbert, Vintage International, New York, pp. 1–46.

Scalia, A. 2005, "Speech at the Juilliard School, in 'Justice Antonin Scalia: In His Own Words'," *BBC News*, February 14, 2016. Available at: www.bbc.com/news/world-us-canada-35571825

Schechter, B. 2007, *The Devil's Own Work: The Civil War Draft Riots and the Fight to Reconstruct America*, Walker Books, New York.

Schopenhauer, A. 2005 [1840], *The Basis of Morality*, trans. A. Bullock, Dover, Mineola, NY.

Sen, A. 2009, *The Idea of Justice*, Harvard University Press, Cambridge, MA.

Seneca, 1928, "On Mercy," in *Moral Essays*, trans. J. Basore, William Heinemann Ltd., London, vol. 1, pp. 356–449.

Shklar, J. 1990, *The Faces of Injustice*, Yale University Press, New Haven, CT.

Solum, L. 1987, "On the Indeterminacy Crisis: Critiquing Critical Dogma," *University of Chicago Law Review*, vol. 54, pp. 462–503.

References 113

Soyinka, W. & Gates, H. L. 2019, "'There's One Humanity or There Isn't': A Conversation," *New York Review of Books*, March 21, pp. 32–34.

Spinoza, B. 1955, *Ethics Preceded by On the Improvement of Understanding*, ed. & trans. J. Gutmann, Hafner Publishing, New York.

Strauss, T. 1942, "Movie Review: Holiday Inn," *New York Times*, August 5. Available at: www.nytimes.com///1942/08/05/archives/the-screen-irving-berlins-holiday-inn-costarring-bing-crosby-and.html?action=click&contentCollection=undefined&region=stream&module=stream_unit&version=latest-stories&contentPlacement=1&pgtype=collection

Tarasoff, v. Regents of the University of California 1976, 17 Cal. 3d 425, 551 P. 2d 334.

Teubner, W. H. 1884, *Ausführliches Lexikon der griechischen und römischen Mythologie*, B. G. Teubner, Leipzig. Available at: https://archive.org/details/ausfhrlicheslexi11rosc/page/512

Thucydides 1961, *The Peloponnesian War*, trans. R. Crawley, Dolphin Books, Garden City, NY.

Torczyner, H. 1977, *Magritte: Ideas and Images*, H. N. Abrams, New York.

Twain, M. 1884, *Adventures of Huckleberry Finn*, Chattow & Windus, London.

Unger, R. M. 1983, *The Critical Legal Studies Movement*, Harvard University Press, Cambridge, MA.

US Department of Justice Policy 2018, "Attorney General Announces Zero-Tolerance Policy for Criminal Illegal Entry," April 6. Available at: www.justice.gov/opa/pr/attorney-general-announces-zero-tolerance-policy-criminal-illegal-entry

van Domselaar, I. 2020, "Law's Regret: On Moral Remainders and a Virtue-Ethical Approach to Legal Decision-Making," *SSRN*, May 18. Available at: https://papers.ssrn.com/sol3/papers.cfm?abstract_id=3604048

van Inwagen, P. & Sullivan, M. 2014, "Metaphysics," *Stanford Encyclopedia of Philosophy*. Available at: https://plato.stanford.edu/entries/metaphysics/

Voltaire 1994, "The ABC, or Dialogues Between ABC (1768)," in A. Williams (ed. & trans.), *Political Writings*, Cambridge University Press, Cambridge, pp. 85–194.

von Ranke, L. 2011, *The Theory and Practice of History*, ed. G. Iggers, Routledge, Milton Park, Abingdon, Oxon.

Warner, E. 1997, "The Translation of Faust," *Deseret Language and Linguistic Society Symposium*, vol. 23(1), pp. 123–27. Available at: https://scholarsarchive.byu.edu/dlls/vol23/iss1/20

Weber, M. 1978, *Economy and Society*, 2 vols., eds. G. Roth & C. Wittich, trans. E. Fischoff et al., University of California Press, Berkeley.

Weber, M. 1976, *The Protestant Ethic and the Spirit of Capitalism*, trans. T. Parsons, Charles Scribner's Sons, New York.

Weber, M. 1958, *From Max Weber: Essays in Sociology*, eds. & trans. H. H. Gerth & C. W. Mills, Oxford University Press, New York.

Weber, M. 1949, *The Methodology of the Social Sciences*, eds. & trans. E. Shils & H. Finch, Macmillan, New York.

Weisberg, K. 1993, *Feminist Legal Theory: Foundations*, Temple University Press, Philadelphia.

Whitman, W. 1950, "Song of Myself," in id, *Leaves of Grass*, Modern Library, New York, pp. 24–74.

114   *References*

Williams, B. 1981, *Moral Luck: Philosophical Papers 1973–1980*, Cambridge University Press, Cambridge.

Williams, B. 1973, "Ethical Consistency," in id, *Problems of the Self: Philosophical Papers 1956–1972*, Cambridge University Press, Cambridge, pp. 166–86.

Wittgenstein, L. 1983, *Remarks on the Foundations of Mathematics*, eds. G. H. von Wright et al., trans. G. E. M. Anscombe, Massachusetts Institute of Technology Press, Cambridge, MA.

Wittgenstein, L. 1978, *Philosophical Grammar*, ed. R. Rhees, trans. A. Kenny, University of California Press, Berkeley.

Wittgenstein, L. 1977, *Culture and Value*, ed. G. H. von Wright, trans. P. Winch, Basil Blackwell, Oxford.

Wittgenstein, L. 1953, *Philosophical Investigations*, trans. G. E. M. Anscombe, Macmillan, New York.

Wolcher, L. 2011, "Asking the Right Question in Business Ethics," *Journal of Law, Business and Ethics*, vol. 17, pp. 9–22.

Index

Note: Page locators in *italics* indicate a figure on the corresponding page.

Absolute Idea 7, 11
act: choosing to 6, 13, 24; of interpretation 30–31, 54–55; of speech 15, 16
Adorno, Theodor: ethics of distanced nearness 34, 37; *Minima Moralia: Reflections from a Damaged Life* 5; morality, theory of 10, 21, 28–29; *Negative Dialects* 10; reason, concept of 5–6, 56–57
American Bar Association (ABA) 1, 2, 96
Angel of History 58
Aquinas, Thomas 27, 75, 84–85
Arendt, Hannah 53, 54
Aristotle: theorist, ethical 2
Arouet, Francois-Marie (Voltaire) 9
Austin, John 75
Axiom of Legal Process: defined 8, 62; noncontroversial, as 9, 66, 85; right, as in doing 67–68, 90

Balkin, Jack 78
Benjamin, Walter 40, 58, 70, 78, 89, 95
Bentham, Jeremy 2, 21, 80
Berger, Peter 90
big fish/little fish concept 11
Boethius, Anicius Manlius Severinus (Boethius) 27, 28
Bonhoeffer, Dietrich 50
Bouwsma, Oets Kolk 38
Buber, Martin 49
burden of caring: compassion of *(Mitleid)* 49–50; concept of 47, 51; egoicity/justification of 48–49, 52;

feeling torn 44–45, 52–53; unwilled ethical impulse 46, 50, 59
Burgo, Bettina 59

Camus, Albert 8
Cantú, Francisco 30
Carson, Anne 18
categorical imperative 1, 6
Chekhov, Anton 20
codes of conduct: ethical 2–3, 62; professional 3, 24, 62, 82
coercion 68, 71, 84
compassion: feelings of 12, 45, 51, 57; mood of 54; reasonable 11, 17, 40; unreasonable feelings of 10–11, 41, 44
Cournot, Antoine-Augustin 66
Cover, Robert 74
Critchley, Simon 104
Critical Legal Studies (CLS) 97–98, 100, 104
criticism, motivation for 63–64

deconstruction 98–100, 104
Derrida, Jacques 58, 78, 98–100
Descartes, René 17, 18; Cartesian theory 18, 99
duty/duties: ethical 23–24, 41, 51, 53, 82; legal 9, 23, 81, 83; moral 12, 23, 57, 61–63, 78–83, 102
Dworkin, Ronald 75, 100

emotion, as untrustworthy 11, 25, 54–55, 57, 80
Encyclopedia of Philosophy 12, 59

116 *Index*

End of History and the Last Man 66
ethical: command 3, 13; compassion, dictates of 10–11; duties 2; norms 11, 13, 16, 26, 29, 36, 46, 56, 58, 61; presponsibilty 60–61; thought 5
ethics: deontological 2, 4, 20, 34; *ethōs* 24–25, 27, 29, 36; of law and politics 12, 59, 92; negative 11, 61; normative 57, 58, 67; philosophical 12; rational 11, 18; teleological 2, 4, 34, 66; virtue 2, 4, 25
Ethics of Deconstruction, The 104
ethics writ large: compassion, *versus* reason 50, 56, 61–64; confidence within 89, 92–93; language theory of 27; moral responsibility to self/other 31–34; untruth of identity 21
ethics writ small: compassion, at war with reason 41–42, 44, 57, 59, 61–62, 67; duty or obligation, defined as 1–2, 62, 64; moral obligation of 23, 90; rational absolute 18, 21
Ewing, Alfred Cyril 39

Faust Part One 14
Finnis, John 82
Fischl, Richard 104
Foucault, Michel 3, 4
freedom: individual 2; moral 52
Fugitive Slave Act 70, 75
Fukuyama, Francis 66
Fuller, Lon 68, 75, 80, 81, 83

Gearey, Adam 105
God: belief in 9, 17, 36, 83; creation, continuous 15; goodness of 60, 86; word of 14
Gods Must Be Crazy, The 31, 32, 38
Goethe, Johann Wolfgang von 14, 18, 29, 34, 55
Gramsci, Antonio 94n13
Grossman, Vasily 11, 59

Hart, Herbert Lionel Adolphus (H.L.A.) 13, 75, 78, 81, 101
Hegel, Georg Wilhelm Friedrich: absolute truth 36; *Philosophy of Right* 18; reason's interpretation of

Self 18; *Sittlichkeit,* ethics concept 36–37, 57, 66; theory of real and ideal 7, 10, 38
Heidegger, Martin: *Befindlichkeit,* theory of existential truth 54, 99; human being, concept of 99; Self, perspective of 28, 47–49
Heinze, Eric 91
Heraclitus 7, 24, 34–36
Herodotus 24
Hesiod 24, 46
Hobbes, Thomas 2
Holmes, Oliver Wendell 16
Hume, David 51, 52
Husserl, Edmund 28
Hyppolite, Jean 42

impulse: ethical 46, 57; revolutionary 63–64; truth 63–64
infinite, nature of 17–19, 60–61
injustice: normalcy of 85; recognizing 17, 68
interpretation: of ethics 6, 38, 50, 68; of justice 71, 83–84; of law, 80, 83; of reality, 10, 18, 37, 54, 104; of reason 46, 66
intuition: categorical 6–7, 21, 41; moral 18, 51–52
Is/Ought 25, 27–29, 31–38, 40, 44–46, 58, 75, 86

Janus 68
Jastrow, Joseph 101
Jefferson, Thomas 87
justice: as blameless 68; blind hope for 65–66, 67; concept of 83; history, end of 66; injustice and 69, 73, *77,* 82–83, 91; theory of 4, 6, 89

Kafka, Franz 69
Kant, Immanuel: Categorical Imperative 6, 8, 12, 15, 21n5, 27, 42; morality, thoughts on 52–53, 60; philosophy of 5–6, 12, 17, 20, 44, 64; theorist 1, 2; *Third Antinomy* 52
Kierkegaard, Søren 23
knowledge, *a priori* 6, 11, 84

La Trahison des images 95, *96*
lawless liberty 2–4, 11, 41

Index 117

legal: actors 62, 77, 82, 99, 104; critical legal studies, movement 81, 97, 104; language 95, 97; norm/normalcy 2, 4, 33, 73, 76, 84; order 70, 73, 76, 89, 104; positivism 75–77, 79–80, 84; positivist 76–78, 82; rules 3, 74, 77, 97–98, 100–1; system 2, 9, 16, 62, 66, 68, 72–74, 82, 95, 97
Leibniz, Gottfried Wilhelm 15, 48, 84
Levinas, Emmanuel 18, 41, 57–61, 91
Lincoln, Abraham 85, 86
linguistic: signs 13, 16, 54–55, 92; socio- 32, 38–40
Locke, John 2, 3, 78
Luckmann, Thomas 90

Maimon, Moses ben (Maimonides) 61
Mannheim, Karl 88
Marxist 10, 33, 88
Marx, Karl 10, 63, 78, 83, 88
Me-Myself 29–30, 56, 64, 93
metaphysical absolutism 36
metaphysics 16, 35, 38, 48, 51, 92
Mill, John Stuart 78
Milosz, Czeslaw 30
moral duty 12, 23, 57, 61–63, 78–83, 102
morality: compassion, as basis for 12; individual 5, 52–53; legal 29, 37, 81; self-criticism of reason 5, 11, 21; subjective 36–37, 39–40, 42
moral remainder 21

Nietzsche, Friedrich 12, 37, 65, 83, 90, 92
norm/norms: ethical 5, 11, 13, 16, 26, 29, 36, 46. 56–58; legal 2, 33–34, 40, 73, 84; moral 24, 26
Nozick, Robert 78

obligation 1, 23–24, 78, 80–82, 83
Oppen, George 52, 54
optimism 65, 68, 84
Orwell, George, *Animal Farm* 7
Oughts 31, 33, 37, 45, 56, 69

Parmenides of Elea 35, 36, 38
Pascal, Blaise 60, 69, 70–71, 73, 85, 91
Patrick, George 84
Péguy, Charles 15

Pindar 23, 35, 89, 99
Plato 12, 25, 35
power, legal 3, 72–73
presponsibility, notion of 57–61, 105
professional: code of conduct 1, 3, 20, 24, 62, 82; ethics 55, 61; responsibility 1, 61–62

Ranke, Leopold von 31
Rawls, John 78
Raz, Joseph 81–83
reason 11; critical 19, 21, 42, 45; disillusioned perspective of 10, 19; interpretation of 46; practical 6, 11, 18–19, 26, 40, 42, 52; qua/intuition 51, 63; relationship between self/other 18; self-criticism of 5–6, 11, 21; speculative 19, 75
Rorty, Richard 99
Rousseau, Jean-Jacques 12, 47

Scalia, Antonin 95
Schopenhauer, Arthur 12, 17, 49–50
Self and Other 5, 15, 18–19, 28, 38, 50, 60
self-certainty 10, 17, 82
self-criticism 5–6, 11, 21
self-interest 11, 12, 78
self-regarding rational ethicist 23, 41
Sen, Amartya 89, 90
Sittlichkeit (ethical life) 8, 36–37, 57, 66
Soyinka, Wole 65
Spinoza, Baruch 12, 36, 38
suffering: another human's 7, 12, 16, 19–20, 58, 61, 63–64; legal 90; needless, avoidable 29, 62
superiority 12, 45, 57

Them/Us 29–30
theology 15, 59, 61, 92
theory: legal 3, 96, 99; rational 21, 90
thought: embracing 17, 72, 95, 99; empty 5, 64
Thucydides 92
treachery: ambiguity of 101–2; of images 95, *96*, 99, 100, 103
truth: absolute self-certainty 16; impulse 63–64; self-evidently 8, 31, 42, 66

118   *Index*

Tuskegee syphilis experiment 58
Twain, Mark 44

unethical 3, 4–5, 21, 57
Unger, Roberto 78
U.S. Constitution 75, 82–83
utilitarianism 20

values: conflicting 21; moral 83
virtue: ethics 2, 4, 25; human 25

Warner, Emily 14
Weber, Max 32, 34, 62, 68, 72–73, 84
Whitman, Walt 24
Williams, Bernard 21
Wittgenstein, Ludwig: absolute
   metaphysical statements, as
   nonsensical 38; aspect-blind theory
   101–3; good, translation of 38–40;
   language, theory of 16, 27, 55, 80
words and deeds 14

Ingram Content Group UK Ltd.
Milton Keynes UK
UKHW022110040523
421267UK00006B/51